CU00704570

'In *God in Public*, Tom Wright draw
member of the House of Lords ar.
biblical scholars to produce a compelling book that speaks to everyone
who wants to engage, biblically and intelligently, with some of the
most pressing issues, both national and international, of our day.'
Baroness Cox, House of Lords

'The "return" of God to public life – some of us think he never
actually left – has taken many people by surprise, and produced a
great deal of nuanced analysis (as well as a fair share of nonsense).
What we have been lacking until now, however, is a robust and
thoughtful biblical critique of this phenomenon: what it means and
how we should respond. Few could have done this with the depth
and fluency of Tom Wright and those familiar with his work will not
be disappointed. *God in Public* is essential reading for those who want
to navigate our changing landscape by drawing on, rather than ignoring, the map and compass that the Bible offers us.'
Nick Spencer, Director of Research at Theos, the Christian think tank

'Religious illiteracy leaves us badly prepared for a world in which
billions believe in and "do" God – and where religion can be used as
a powerful force for good or ill. *God in Public*'s hard-edged realism
never lapses into backward-looking nostalgia, providing charts and
maps for treacherous and dangerous waters. Tom Wright's message is
authentic and urgent. Whether you come from a secular or believing
background, *God in Public* has important things to say to you.'
Lord Alton of Liverpool, House of Lords

Tom Wright is Research Professor of New Testament and Early Christianity at the University of St Andrews. He is the author of over seventy books, including the For Everyone guides to the New Testament and, most recently, *Creation, Power and Truth, Finding God in the Psalms, The Meal Jesus Gave Us, Surprised by Scripture, Simply Good News* and *Paul and the Faithfulness of God* (all published by SPCK).

GOD IN PUBLIC

How the Bible speaks truth
to power today

TOM WRIGHT

First published in Great Britain in 2016

Society for Promoting Christian Knowledge
36 Causton Street
London SW1P 4ST
www.spck.org.uk

Copyright © Nicholas Thomas Wright 2016

All rights reserved. No part of this book may be reproduced or transmitted in any
form or by any means, electronic or mechanical, including photocopying,
recording, or by any information storage and retrieval system,
without permission in writing from the publisher.

SPCK does not necessarily endorse the individual views contained in its publications.

Scripture quotations are either taken from the New Revised Standard Version of the
Bible, Anglicized Edition, copyright © 1989, 1995 by the Division of Christian
Education of the National Council of the Churches of Christ in the USA,
used by permission, all rights reserved; or are the author's own translation,
with most taken from *The New Testament for Everyone* by Tom Wright,
copyright © Nicholas Thomas Wright 2011.
One quotation is from the Authorized Version of the Bible (The King James Bible),
the rights in which are vested in the Crown, and is reproduced by permission
of the Crown's Patentee, Cambridge University Press.

British Library Cataloguing-in-Publication Data
A catalogue record for this book is available from the British Library

ISBN 978–0–281–07423–5
eBook ISBN 978–0–281–07424–2

Typeset by Graphicraft Limited, Hong Kong
First printed in Great Britain by Ashford Colour Press
Subsequently digitally printed in Great Britain

eBook by Graphicraft Limited, Hong Kong

Produced on paper from sustainable forests

To Andrew and Lis Goddard

Contents

Contents

Preface

As I look back over the last twenty years, I find that I have increasingly been concerned with the question of how to speak about God in the public forum. Much of my early training and formation had taken it for granted that my task as a biblical scholar and priest would be to teach the church how to read the Bible and live Christianly, and the only thing to say to the 'outside world' would be a summons to repent and believe in Jesus.

The middle years of my ministry – first as a dean in a busy cathedral, then as a canon of Westminster, then as Bishop of Durham with a seat in the House of Lords – compelled me to address all sorts of questions about faith and public life. These had not, up to that point, impinged very much on my thinking, let alone on my reading of the Bible – though my study of Jesus in particular had paved the way. Once you start to understand what he meant by the kingdom of God, these questions cannot be put off much longer. This book is a small sample of the things I have found myself saying as a result.

There is a sense in which these pieces, too, are about the call to repent and believe in Jesus, but in a much larger sphere and sense. They have to do with society and culture as a whole rather than simply the challenge to individuals. (Despite what I sometimes hear said, I firmly believe that every single person must face that challenge for themselves. We cannot hide behind a societal or corporate vision.) Jesus warned his contemporaries to read the signs of the times; his message was addressed to whole cities and his whole culture, not just one person here and another there. This is either a message for the whole world or it is meaningless. Jesus claimed, at the end of Matthew's gospel (28.18), that 'all authority in heaven *and on earth*' had been given to him. I have been trying to discern – and express – something of what that might mean in our own day.

One of the 'signs of our times' is precisely that addressing the wider world with the Christian message is difficult and contentious. We have lived for a long time in an implicit split-level universe where 'God', if there is such a being, is detached from this world, leaving us to fend for ourselves (and perhaps go and visit him on Sundays).

People sometimes speak as if this split is the inevitable result of modern scientific knowledge, but that is simply a mistake: the idea of a split-level world, with God or the gods a long way away, is ancient Epicureanism, revived for other reasons in modern Western Europe and then used as a frame by some scientists (not all) to display their findings. All that is a topic for another time, though it is important to see how something which our culture often takes for granted is itself the product of special interests and, often, special pleading.

My point here is, the pieces that make up the present book are some of my varied attempts to bring together the message of Jesus – in its larger biblical context – and the challenges of the contemporary public and political worlds. In some cases I was speaking to fellow Christians *about* this task and what it might look like. In some others – such as the lecture at the London School of Economics – I was actually trying to *do* it. In several cases I think it was a bit of both.

A book like this is bound to repeat itself. One could, indeed, turn it into a different sort of book, taking the various themes that over-lap and recur and expounding them systematically, but that would then require a larger framework and the joining of a good many dots. I hope the effect will be that of adding more and more clarifying layers by covering similar topics, but from different angles. I hope, too, that the sense of a vivid, immediate presentation will come through. I have lively memories of all the different occasions and am very grateful to those who invited me to address them, organized the occasions and provided hospitality (a full list is given in the Acknowledgements at the back).

This book is dedicated to Andrew and Lis Goddard. Friends and colleagues over several decades, they have helped me to see the many ways in which the gospel has an impact on both public and private life. Their fellowship and support have meant a great deal to me and my family.

Tom Wright
St Mary's College
St Andrews

1

Paul and the Bible in tomorrow's world

Three images bring into focus the question of 'God in Public'.

First, I think of Prime Minister Tony Blair in the aftermath of September 11, 2001, hastily reading the Qur'an to find out what was going on. Better late than never, you might suppose; but if we were to imagine the opposite picture, of an Iraqi or Afghan leader reading the New Testament to find out why the 'Christian' West was bombing his country, we might realize that things are a little more complicated than that.

Second, take the controversy in the UK a few years ago about the government's decision to do away with funding for second degrees if they were not at a higher level than the first. That might look innocuous: a technical detail tidied up, you might think. But among the many unintended consequences of such a move was that candidates for the ordained ministry, who were intending to study theology as a second degree, would not be eligible for funding, thus putting a sudden large burden on the church. The bishops naturally protested about this; but the public reaction was the really interesting thing. Some Christians said that ministers don't need to study theology; they just need to know their Bibles and to be inspired by the Spirit, and that academic theology would just confuse them and their flocks. Some non-Christians have said that theology ought not in any case to be taught at universities. Some expressed surprise that it was still regarded as a serious subject, attributing its continuance to the inertia of the long-outdated Establishment.

Third, I think of the stridently secular British weekly *New Statesman*. Remarkably enough for such a publication, in 2009 it commissioned a special report entitled 'God: What Do We Believe?' (This followed a similar special issue of *The Economist*.) Sadly, most of the articles were trite and obvious. The only overtly Christian contributor was the Conservative politician Ann Widdecombe, and she was only allowed three sentences. In much of the material one got the sense that the *New Statesman* knew there was a question there to be addressed but wasn't quite sure what it was. There was, however, one thoughtful piece, by Sholto Byrnes, pointing out that our new moralities of scientific certainty, human rights and ecology, just as strident and self-righteous as any puritan preacher, constituted a secular form of an earlier vision of God and his purposes, and that without that vision they were actually baseless.

We could go on. One of the great traditions of English cities is the ringing of church bells. In many places this is simply taken for granted (though newcomers sometimes protest). But not long ago a controversy raged in Oxford about whether the Muslim call to prayer should also be allowed to echo around the dreaming spires. If churches can wake people up with their bells, why not mosques with their chanting? But, more widely, it wouldn't be difficult to argue that the crisis in Western democracy is itself a symptom of a deeper malaise. (If you don't think there's a crisis in Western democracy, pause for a moment and ask yourself what actually goes on in Westminster . . . or, for that matter, what on earth is going on in the United States, as billions of dollars are spent on obtaining votes in an arcane system which can be cynically manipulated – and all this when the UK and USA are trying to suggest to the rest of the world that if only they all became liberal democrats like us then everything would be all right.) There is a deep uncertainty about who we are and what we're here for, and I suggest that this malaise is directly linked to the banishing of God from the public square two hundred years ago. But before we pursue all this any further, we need to call a witness from the ancient home of democracy.

In Acts 17 we find St Paul, a highly intelligent Jew who believes that Jesus of Nazareth is the Lord of the world, standing before the highest court in Athens. He's been in Athens a few days and he's made a dangerous impression. People think he's been talking about 'foreign divinities', because he's been going on about Jesus and the Resurrection, *Iēsous kai anastasis*, and they think that *Anastasis* is a female divinity, perhaps the consort of this Jesus. But that's not simply a curiosity; it's a potential capital charge. As everyone knew, the two charges against Socrates were that he was corrupting the young and that he was preaching foreign divinities. So it isn't merely intellectual curiosity that has caused Paul to be dragged to the Areopagus and told to explain himself. Foreign divinities, and chattering his strange and possibly subversive ideas in the marketplace to all and sundry! This is serious stuff. And already I can hear echoes in our very different but strangely similar world, as our new moralities have translated into secularizing law. Famously, a few years ago, an airline worker was sacked because she insisted on wearing a cross. Meanwhile, her Muslim counterpart in France was prohibited from wearing her headdress. This goes closely with the strident polemic of people like Richard Dawkins, who has declared that to bring a child up 'religious' is worse than physical abuse. Religion – at least religions within the Abrahamic traditions, that make uncomfortably absolute claims in a world where the one thing we can't tolerate is intolerance – is a disturbing presence, perhaps a dangerous presence. Perhaps, people think, it should be banned altogether. So it was with Paul's new ideas in Athens. He faced being run out of town, or quite possibly worse.

The framework for our question is not, obviously, the same as it was for him. But let's pause anyway, and contemplate where we are and how we got there, before letting the apostle have his say. Today in the Western world we are living with a major stand-off between what we might loosely call fundamentalism and secularism. The events of September 11, 2001 precipitated the particular form of this stand-off, as the secularists have been able to point to horrible things done in the name of 'religion'. But the religious can give as good as they get on that one, with the horrors of secularism stretching from the guillotine in Paris to the Soviet Gulag and beyond. And in fact these are only small symptoms of the ways in which Western society has split apart. This has been going on ever since the Enlightenment banished God into the private sphere, like a demented elderly relative confined to the attic: we can visit him from time to time, but he mustn't be allowed to come downstairs and embarrass us, especially when there are visitors present.

That split between religion and real life has been written into the constitution of some countries, such as France and the United States of America, albeit with radically different results; and there are many in our own country who wish we could not only make the split absolute ourselves but also, by some form of ideological euthanasia, get rid of the old boy upstairs altogether. And, from having spent half my adult life in academic institutions, I wouldn't be altogether surprised to learn that there are some who might like to turn university and college chapels into concert halls, to stop teaching theology, and to banish all signs of God from public student life, much as in the USA some people are trying to erase the words 'In God We Trust' from the dollar bill.

Part of the heat in the secularist agenda comes from the frustration that the secularization myth hasn't run according to plan. Religion was supposed to have withered on the vine by now, but not only is Islam growing and in some cases threatening, but Christianity is making a come-back – not just in far-off lands where we can patronizingly suppose the locals to be less civilized, less 'enlightened', than ourselves, but also in the UK. The secularists love to quote statistics of decline in church membership, but they can't understand why attendance at major services such as Christmas has been steadily growing. Postmodernism, in deconstructing all big narratives, has deconstructed the secular one as well, and suddenly people who'd been starved of spirituality for far too long are rediscovering it, albeit often without being able to explain what it is they want or how it relates to the classic claims of the Christian faith. This puzzle is one of the major forces shaping tomorrow's world. If we are to have anything to say in that world we must learn to think and speak clearly about it.

Two other things are going on in our world which feed off one another and help create the climate within which the ancient question of God in public must be addressed today and tomorrow. I'm just going to mention them briefly here, because they are both whole subjects in themselves; but I don't think we can understand where we are without them. Very briefly, they are Gnosticism and empire. (I discuss this more fully in *Creation, Power and Truth* (London: SPCK, 2013).) For Gnosticism, think of Dan Brown's famous novel *The Da Vinci Code*, and ask yourself why it has been so massively popular. It's all about conspiracy theories, one within the next like a series of Russian dolls. In fact, in the book, history itself, and indeed the church itself, turns out to be a conspiracy, with the 'hidden truth' about Jesus and Mary Magdalene suppressed by the church and now emerging from 'freshly discovered ancient documents'. And this 'hidden truth' then points back to supposed hidden truths about ourselves: that the secret of the universe is within us, that we have a spark of the divine deep down inside, and the aim is to be true to that spark, to follow that star wherever it leads, to reject outward forms and historically grounded faith and to escape the constraints of the world into a timeless spiritual sphere. Some people even suppose this is what true Christianity is all about, but in fact it is very nearly its opposite. It is, however, the religion of at least a third of the movies made in Hollywood. You only have to hint at it to have people buying your books by the barrowload.

And Gnosticism flourishes within empire: because when people sense that the world is run by very rich and very powerful people, and there's nothing they can do about it, they tend to shrug their shoulders and suppose they'd better turn inwards, away from the public sphere. And, naturally, empires want people to do that. To that extent, Marx got it spot on. Religion (of a certain sort) is there to keep the masses quiet, to assure them of spiritual peace in the present and spiritual bliss in the future, so long as the rich and powerful can go on carving up the world to their advantage. The irony is that it is now our supposed Western democracies that are dividing up the world and making a large profit, as they pursue the rhetorical agenda of freedom, justice and peace by the age-old means of enslavement, bullying and war. (If you think that is overstating the point, or that I am merely collapsing into a left-wing rant, think again.) And the rhetoric of democracy itself conveniently masks the reality of tyranny: we are (so we suppose) the enlightened ones; we vote every four or five years; so we claim the moral high ground from which we can exploit, harass and ultimately bomb to smithereens those who haven't attained our level of civilization, and who, conveniently, haven't yet attained our level of weaponry (and we use high-flown moral arguments to tell them they're naughty to want to). Tomorrow's world will be dominated by these confusions, and if the Christian gospel can bring not only clarity but a fresh sense of direction we should all be grateful.

Let's sum up where we've got to so far. The current stand-off between fundamentalism and secularism is shot through with at least these three other elements, postmodernity, Gnosticism and empire, which bounce off one another. And the question of God in public has to be addressed with our ears attuned to these surging impulses, and to the way in which the issues of our day come with an inescapable God-dimension which, if you try to deny it, will merely return to haunt you in dangerous ways. These are the forces shaping tomorrow's world.

So let's return to Paul in Athens. Athens knew a lot about democracy and empire, and indeed about Gnosticism and other types of religion. Let's see if what Paul said there has resonances which will help us speak wisely of God, and indeed act wisely for God, in tomorrow's dangerous and confusing public world.

Paul has two things to say which echo round the debating halls of Athens and right on into our own day. The first is the existence of *the unseen but present creator God*. This is the foundation of all classic Jewish and Christian thought, and it cuts across ideologies today just as it cut through Athenian philosophies then. Let me tell you, says Paul, about the God you acknowledge vaguely with your 'altar to the unknown God'. That altar was a kind of open end in the Athenian worldview, a question mark amid the confusion of polytheism: perhaps we've forgotten someone, perhaps there *is* something more. Yes, says Paul, there is; and I'm here to tell you about it.

The three main worldview options then were the Stoic, the Epicurean and the Academic (the latter being a type of Platonism, which was itself in flux). The Stoics basically said that God and the world were the same thing, so that what you had to do was to get in touch with the inner *logos* or reason within yourself and the world. The Epicureans said that the gods were totally other than the world, and very far away from it, so that the thing to do was to acknowledge them at a distance and carve out your own life as best you could. That, interestingly, was the basic theme of the eighteenth-century Enlightenment, and it remains a prevalent view today. The Academics said there wasn't really enough evidence to be sure about all that stuff, but that we'd better keep the old religious customs going just in case – a position not unknown, alas, within the Church of England. Meanwhile the general populace sacrificed in the temples, kept the festivals, and invoked every god or goddess that they thought might be of some use. It was just as much a complex scene as ours is. Any attempt to flatten out either Paul's setting or our own will make a nonsense of it all.

So watch how Paul navigates the Athenian scene with his Jewish message about the unseen but present creator God. It's clear, he says, that you're a very religious people, but actually all these splendid temples you have – think of them, the Parthenon, the Temple of Nike, and so on, some of the greatest architectural achievements in all human civilization – they're actually a category mistake. The God who made the world doesn't live in houses like that. Nor does he need people to come and give him dead animals to eat. And then Paul shows, quoting from local poets, that the God who made the heavens and the earth is unseen but present. The Stoics had it half right: divinity is indeed near at hand, there are signs of it all around; but they had it half wrong, imagining that divinity was simply contained within all things. Rather, the creator remains sovereign over, and other than, the world he's made, even though he's filled it with signs of his power and glory. So too the Epicureans had it half right: God is not the same thing as the world. But they had it half wrong, imagining that therefore God and the world were at a great distance from one another. Rather, the creator remains intimately close to the world, and particularly to human beings, 'not far from each one of us', because 'in him we live and move and have our being', and he longs for us to feel out in the dark and find him there.

So what about the Academics? Well, Paul has news for them, and this is where his second point comes in, which is *God's action to put the world to rights*. This God, intimately present though mysteriously unseen, has put down a fresh marker within the world. The Academics too had it half right, in that up to now things have been obscure and uncertain. There has been a level of ignorance. The true God is aware of that, and he isn't holding people responsible for it. But now this same creator God is sending out a message to all and sundry to turn around from the way they were going and come his way instead. He is calling the world to account, promising to put all wrongs to right, to sort out the mess and bring the world into a new harmony. (Notice how Paul is stealing the court's thunder. They think they're the highest court in the land, but Paul is telling them that there's a higher one still, and that they are accountable to it.)

And here comes the point for which they were totally unprepared, the point which explains everything else, the point which still bursts as an embarrassment on to the polite discussions of religion and ethics, of philosophy and government. God has fixed a day, declares Paul, on which he will judge the world with true justice, and he will do so *through a man whom he has appointed*; and he has given assurance of this by raising him from the dead. Jesus and Anastasis, Jesus and the resurrection: *that's* what he had been talking about in the marketplace, that is the announcement which was going to get him into trouble, that is the message that he's now set in its proper context.

7

You can't fit Jesus and the resurrection into pagan worldviews as though they're just two more miscellaneous divinities. You have to understand them within the essentially Jewish worldview in which there is one single creator God who remains intimately involved with the world, one single God who will at the last put the world to rights. That Jewish worldview has come sharply into focus, Paul declares, in the events concerning Jesus.

And particularly his resurrection. For Paul, the resurrection wasn't (as it is in some systems today, including fundamentalism) a bizarre miracle which shows that God is a powerful supernatural being and that there is a life after death. For Paul, the resurrection of Jesus was the beginning of the new creation, the moment when the creator God revealed that in Jesus the power of chaos, entropy and death itself had been defeated and that a new world of genuine justice and peace was opening up. God was putting the world to rights already, by the message of the gospel opening hearts and minds and communities to a new way of being human, ahead of the time when he would eventually sort the whole lot out in a final act of judgment and mercy. The resurrection of Jesus makes no sense within other worldviews, but within this one it becomes the prototypical event, the thing which reveals what everything else is about, and where it's going. (Resurrection, interestingly, was ruled out, as far as the Areopagus was concerned, by divine fiat. According to ancient legend, Apollo himself had declared, as the court of the Areopagus was being founded, that once a person had died, and their blood was spilled on the ground, there was no resurrection. Oh yes there is, declares Paul, because Apollo doesn't have the last word. The last word belongs to the creator God, the God who will put the whole world to rights, the God revealed in Jesus and his resurrection.)

That is fighting talk, in the first century or the twenty-first. And let's get one thing straight before we ask how this same gospel challenge plays out in tomorrow's world. I've heard people say often enough that we can't believe in the resurrection today because modern science has disproved it. That is ridiculous: we didn't have to wait for Newton and Leibniz, for the Industrial Revolution or the invention of penicillin, to discover that when people die they stay dead. Homer and Plato knew that just as well as we do. What has happened, rather, is that the rhetoric of the Enlightenment needed to be able to say that human history had been blundering along in ignorance until the eighteenth century and was now at last coming out into the light, justifying whatever Western Europe and North America then wanted to do by way of social ordering and empire. That is actually a parody of the Christian claim Paul makes in his speech in Athens: up to now, it's been shadows and puzzles, but now we have a new revelation! And for the new story of the Enlightenment to stick, the old one had to be got out of the way. There cannot be two climaxes to world history: if it's us, it can't be Jesus. And that in turn gives us the clue to our own question.

For some, to mention the resurrection at all looks like fundamentalism. And certainly the secularist will want nothing to do with it. But the fundamentalist inhabits a dualistic universe, where you reject the goodness of this creation and try to escape to another world altogether, with the resurrection merely as the sign of a supernatural power that helps you to do that. But for the early Christians the resurrection was the launching-point of new creation itself, renewing the world rather than abandoning it, affirming its goodness and beauty and power out the other side of the judgment that falls on its corruption and decay. I have a sense that most Western Christians have yet to wake up to what the resurrection means in practice: those who believe in it don't understand it, and those who don't believe it don't want it. As Jim Wallis said in his book *God's Politics*, the right gets it wrong and the left doesn't get it. (He was writing about US politics, but the same goes for theology, and the two are intimately interconnected.)

In particular, the resurrection challenges those three powerful currents of human life and thought which are shaping tomorrow's world, namely Gnosticism, empire and postmodernity. The resurrection declares that true spirituality is world-renewing, not world-renouncing: God's kingdom is not *from* this world but it certainly is *for* this world. Instead of the escape route of the Gnostic, the private spirituality which detaches itself from the world in the present and seeks to leave it altogether in the future, the New Testament offers the integrated spirituality which knows that when the sign of the cross hangs over the world in its distorted, twisted pain and shame, that is so that the resurrection can bring it to life both in the ultimate future, in the new heavens and new earth, and in the penultimate future, as God's life-giving power is unleashed in works of justice and mercy and healing and beauty and hope already, in the present. The Gnostic, like the fundamentalist, can never understand why we Christians are called to work for justice and health in the present world, but with the resurrection there is no question. Of course we are.

And that is the basis, too, of the Christian challenge to empire, to the arrogance which assumes that we (whoever 'we' are: it was 'we British' a hundred years ago, it's the Americans now, it will be someone else before too long) innately possess justice, freedom and peace and have the right to bestow them on others, by force if necessary. The thing about empires is that ultimately they rule by the power of fear, whose end is death. And one of the reasons why the empires of the world try to suppress or subvert the news of Jesus' resurrection is because if Jesus has overcome death itself then the power of the tyrant is broken. That is why theology that colludes with empire has always been eager to say that the resurrection isn't really a 'historical' event, in case after all God came out of his private attic and started to be relevant in the public world, the real world, the world of economics and law, of business and climate change, of the Middle East and of Middle England, of cities and slums and scandals and sleaze.

Because the resurrection of Jesus of Nazareth is the fixed point from which we must start again in our thinking and living amid the swirling sands of postmodernity. And for this reason: the postmodernist deconstructs all grand narratives, declaring that they are stories which get people into power and keep them there. But the resurrection of *Jesus* – the real Jesus, the one who healed the sick and loved the poor and died on the cross – is not a power story; it's a love story. It offers a different kind of truth, not brittle and fragile like the truth-claims of the fundamentalist or the secularist, but supple and strong and capable of taking on the world. Tomorrow's world. Tomorrow's public world.

So what might it look like to 'do God in public' with the message of Jesus and the resurrection? To be sure, such a vision must be rooted in worship and prayer. Without that, we will turn even the finest truth into a self-serving ideology, or collapse it into a cacophony of mere slogans. We've been there quite enough already. But genuine worship and prayer, including sacraments and the reading of scripture, must issue in resurrection living. Let me give you, as I close, three snapshots of what it might look like in this way to 'do God in public' in tomorrow's world.

Come with me, first, round the corner from a downtown church on Teesside. It's four in the morning and there's a steady drizzle in the darkness. Four or five people are waiting by the road. Then a bus pulls up, and out get twenty-five confused and frightened people. They have come to the UK seeking asylum, often at the risk of their lives. The British government has treated them like semi-criminals, and shipped them off to the other end of the country in the dark. But the church has got wind of it and is waiting for them, waiting to welcome them, to give them food and shelter, to hear their stories and see what they can do to help. And the church will stand with them at the tribunal, will help them fill in forms and make applications and find somewhere to live and become part of the community. And the church will also, boldly and without fear, speak up for them, and against the policies which criminalize and still threaten them, and the church will do this everywhere from the local pub all the way up – or is it down? – to the House of Lords. That is 'doing God in public', and it provokes, I have discovered, exactly the same reaction that Paul got in Athens.

Second, there was a nice irony in that issue of the *New Statesman* I mentioned earlier. On the inside of the front cover was an advertisement for the Salvation Army. It was headed 'Belief in Action'. That page offered a far more powerful statement of God in public than any of the articles in the official feature which was supposed to be dealing with that subject. While the commentariat chatters about theoretical possibilities, the church is out in the street addressing the problems. Again and again, when the church is doing what Jesus did, bringing the saving rule of God to the homeless, to young people at risk, to the sick and the addicts and the imprisoned, we are seeing what the resurrection is all about: God's world put to rights, in the present, anticipating the ultimate future. Something like three-quarters of all those who do volunteer work in the hundreds of organizations that enable British society to flourish do so from a more or less explicit base of faith. Take that away – banish God to the private realm alone – and it would be shocking to see the things that would disappear with them, specifically a great many signs of healing and hope. You cannot separate the political goods to be pursued by the church and the political goods to be pursued by the world outside the church. Rather, the church is supposed to be the body through which God is addressing and reclaiming the world. And this cannot but be a public activity.

Third, come with me to the debating chambers, whether of Parliament, Congress, or of the United Nations; of the local council or indeed of a university, college or faculty. The major ethical and public–political issues of our day rumble on: global debt, the ecological crisis, the new poverty in our own glossy Western society, the working and meaning of democracy itself, issues of gender and sex, stem cell research, euthanasia, and not least the multiply complex questions of the Middle East. Oh, and 'free speech' too. As long as the debates are carried out in terms of fundamentalism on the one hand and secularism on the other, they will never be anything other than a shouting match.

At this point, ironically, the Enlightenment dream has begun to eat its own tail: its greatest strength, the emphasis on Reason as the means to peaceful coexistence, has been undermined by its greatest weakness, the dualistic division between God and the public world, with human public discourse then collapsing into spin, emotivism and all kinds of attempts to rule out alternative points of view other than the currently 'correct' one. Perhaps part of the unintended consequence of the postmodern revolution is to reveal that if Reason is to do what it says on the tin we may after all need to reckon with God in public. And for that to happen we need wise Christian voices at the table, voices neither strident nor fundamentalist, voices both humble and clear; the voices not of those with instant answers but of those with a fresh grasp of God's truth, whose word will carry conviction because it appeals, like Paul with the altar to the unknown God, to things which everybody half knows but many try to suppress. The rulers of this age need to be called to account, as the former UN General Secretary Kofi Annan insisted in his retirement speech. This must be done, and ultimately can only be done, in the name of the one who will at the last put all things to rights.

These are the voices that we need in tomorrow's world: the voices of those who are doing God in public, who have thought through the issues of the day in the light of the gospel of Jesus, and who can address them, like Paul, with courage and compelling wisdom. And my prayer is that some of those voices will be yours.

2

The Bible and the postmodern world

I had better begin by defining my terms. Most of us are dimly aware that, as someone said recently, 'reality isn't what it used to be'. We are in the middle of enormous cultural changes within Western society, which leave many observers bewildered and many participants bemused. All the signs are that things are going to get more confusing, not less, and that the onset of the millennium, which at one level had nothing to do with postmodernity and all that, made people on the one hand eager for and on the other hand fearful of great changes in the way we look at the world. The so-called 'millennium bug', the nasty cold that all our computers were supposed to catch on 1 January 2000, was, at the level of contemporary mythology, a wonderfully symptomatic disease of postmodernity: explorations into cyberspace that forgot a ruthlessly modernist piece of equipment, so that when the new age dawned they, as with Cinderella on the stroke of midnight, might well have turned into pumpkins.

But, in case some feel left behind by all this jargon, what do we mean by 'modernity' and 'postmodernity', anyway? A quick thumbnail sketch is called for at this point. By the 'modern' world I mean, broadly, the Western world from the eighteenth century to the present. The European Enlightenment at the intellectual level, and the Industrial Revolution at the social level, produced enormous changes both in how society worked, literally and metaphorically, and in how people thought. The large-scale shift from agrarian economies to factory economies had, inevitably, profound social consequences, not only in Europe but in many other countries as far afield as New Zealand. Those who learned to think for themselves in the Enlightenment without fear of tradition – and then, in the Industrial Revolution, those who learned to make things for themselves rather than having to grow them – acquired a new confidence. They could take on the world.

Thus there grew up the modernist trinity: first, the confident individual who says, 'I am the master of my fate, I am the captain of my soul.' Second, there was certainty about the world and about our objective knowledge of it. We can look at the world and know things, and that is objective knowledge. (Someone said that facts, like telescopes and wigs for gentlemen, were an eighteenth-century invention. In fact, both date at least to the seventeenth century, but the point stands: the idea of 'objective truth', of 'hard facts', is a relatively modern invention.) Third, and perhaps above all, there grew up a new mythology of *progress*: the belief that the world was actually going somewhere, was progressing, and was about to reach its goal. Reality was then conveniently divided up into facts and values: facts were objective, values were subjective. Or, in another of the great Enlightenment ways of carving up the world, there were the truths of reason 'out there' which the mind might be able to grasp, and the truths of the actual empirical world, the things that you could actually do business with. There was an ugly ditch, said the German philosopher Lessing, between the two of them. Split-level reality is what the modernist trinity purchased at considerable cost, and we have been paying that cost ever since.

The negative corollaries of all this are quite clear: the European world said that we were no longer bound to traditional religions or ethics. We were now living in the real world, people said, and religion and ethics were a matter of private opinion. Part of the avowed aim of modernity was to get away from endless European wars of religion, by showing that religions were simply about what people did with their solitude, and that it was therefore absurd to fight one another about such beliefs. We have learned to think for ourselves, and we can use this ability to show up barbarity and superstition, to free ourselves from the tyranny of tradition.

It is this heady combination, I think, that people regularly refer to when they talk about 'living in the modern world'. Its positive achievements are obvious: modern medicine, communications, and hundreds of other social improvements. With a few exceptions, such as the Amish community in Pennsylvania, we all live off the modernist achievement. Its darker side is not always so well known, but examples include of course the French Revolution. However much the aristocracy had been asking for it, a movement of 'liberty, equality and brotherhood' that killed thousands of people, including many of its own, to make the point is self-defeating, and hardly a good advertisement for its own principles.

14

Likewise, the myth of progress and enlightenment (which was already there in poets like Keats) created the context not only for Charles Darwin, but for that which followed in his wake, namely 'Social Darwinism'. It was 'Social Darwinism' that made talk of eugenics, racial purity, selective breeding and ultimately 'final solutions' – that is, mass murder and genocide – possible and acceptable, even apparently desirable, not only in Germany but also in the UK and elsewhere. Nor should we forget that those whom the Enlightenment enabled to think of themselves as 'masters of their fate' and 'captains of their souls' were standing on the enslaved shoulders of millions of workers. For the workers, the main effect of swapping agricultural serfdom for industrial wage-slavery was the loss of fresh air.

If we pursue the political point for a moment, there is something else which we need to recall. As Western society has levelled out in the last two hundred years, it has increasingly achieved this freedom at the expense of the rest of the world. The brave new reality of modernity, symbolized by the architecture, music, art and politics of the 1950s and 1960s, has looked increasingly hollow. This is the context for the rise of postmodernity.

Before looking at that phenomenon, though, let us think for a moment of what happened to the Bible within modernity. It was seen, naturally, as part of the tradition that had to be overthrown. In a world where 'objective facts' were what counted, the Bible was weighed in the modernist balance and found wanting. Since Progress, not Creation, was what counted, 'evolution' must be 'right' and 'special creation' must be 'wrong'. Genesis was therefore out of line. Since science studied the unalterable laws of nature, miracles were out of the question, and half the biblical account stood accused of fairy-tale fantasy.

When the so-called Jesus Seminar in California debated the resurrection of Jesus, and then went public with a press conference to announce that they had concluded that the resurrection didn't happen, they brought in as part of their evidence a young woman who worked in a mortuary in Los Angeles. She testified before the press that she worked all the time with dead bodies; and they always stayed dead! This was supposed to be some kind of fresh 'scientific' revelation. But actually that was always part of the point of the resurrection of Jesus. Of course dead people normally stay dead. The point of the resurrection is that something new – new creation, nothing less – has burst upon the world.

So what might all this say about reading the stories of Jesus? According to H. S. Reimarus in the late eighteenth century, Jesus was actually some kind of Galilean revolutionary. So the idea of his being 'the son of man', let alone the son of God, let alone dying and rising for the sins of the world, must have been the pious invention of the later church, on its way to the Constantinian enslavement of the world in religious superstition. (Notice the way in which, at certain points, the Enlightenment borrowed the rhetoric of the Reformation, while firmly rejecting its spiritual certainties.) As for biblical ethics, within modernity they were quite simply out of date. That, you might suppose, is an odd idea to apply to an ethic: do morals change with the calendar? But there it is; and anyone invoking the classic standards of the Jewish and Christian worlds is in danger of being accused of 'Stone Age morality'. Within this modernist context, the Bible is reduced in its public role to being read in the liturgy, where if we're not careful it functions not as a powerful word breaking afresh into human communities, but more as a piece of verbal wallpaper. In its private role, it can be reduced to being read in order to inspire holy thoughts in individuals, which it might do, some would hope, irrespective of its truth-claims. So strong has been the rhetoric of the modernist world-view that any attempt to show that these negative judgments about the Bible were ill-founded has regularly been dismissed as attempting to recreate a bygone age. The tide of modernity is coming in, and anyone who questions it is a fundamentalist Canute.

But, as we all know, the modernist movement has been having an increasingly hard time of it. Marx, Nietzsche and Freud, the masters of suspicion nurtured within the bosom of modernity, propounding their theories as 'scientific' and hence respectable within that frame of reference, have shaken to the core the modernist vision of reality and all that went with it. Again, the briefest of accounts must suffice here.

The context for the cultural change has again been a change in the methods and assumptions of the way we live. A British Telecom advertisement, which urged 'Why Not Change The Way We Work', was, like most good advertisements, telling people to do something they were already beginning to do or to want to do. Instead of all that boring, expensive commuting to your city offices, using up fuel and polluting the atmosphere, why not stay in your comfortable home in the suburbs and do your entire work from a distance? The microchip has replaced the factory, the secretary, and a lot of other things and people as well. Communities that depended on eighteenth-century ways of doing things have been reduced to mass unemployment – or to the status of theme parks: in the UK there are now places where the inhabitants are paid to dress up (as miners, steelworkers or whatever) and do, to amuse the tourists, what their forebears did actually to produce useful products. This phenomenon is a major feature of the British landscape and I suspect of other countries as well. Instead of producing and making things, entertainment is the order of the day.

This industrial and sociological change dovetails neatly into the changed vision of reality that is so characteristic of postmodernity. Instead of objective facts (hard-edged things, like lumps of coal or steel girders) we have impressions, attitudes and feelings, floating around in the cyberspace which all of us visit but few of us could describe accurately. At a conference in Dallas a few years ago I heard a speaker say enthusiastically, 'Today, attitudes are more important than facts – and we can document that!' That was a wonderful statement, trembling on the brink between modernity and postmodernity. We have learned, in the title of a recent book, that 'Truth is stranger than it used to be'; that all truth-claims are made *by* somebody or some group, and we normally assume that the claims are serving the interest of the groups in question. After all, everybody has a set of agendas; and ingenious critics can smoke these out with the help of a street-level wisdom that goes back ultimately to Marx, Nietzsche or Freud.

This is obviously what preoccupies Western journalists, not only when they have a leading politician on the rack but all down the scale. In the British newspapers at least (the USA is sometimes different, it seems) most of the journalists, most of the time, only ever tell one story. The details change, but the story is the same; namely, that all the people who think they are somebody have actually got feet of clay. This applies to bishops, rock stars and politicians alike. The newspapers are not really interested in positive, good-news stories. They are there to cut everyone else down to size.

At least, that is the impression we get from them, over and over again. A few years ago it emerged that the reforms undertaken at Westminster Abbey had resulted in the regular worshipping congregation multiplying to four times its previous size. One result of this was that the annual Christmas tree, a gift from Her Majesty the Queen, had to be moved from its normal spot to make room for all the people coming to pray and sing Christmas carols. This was reported in the London *Times*, however – on the front page! – not as a story about the growth of a vibrant worshipping community, but as a story about the Dean of Westminster offering a snub to Her Majesty. People often say 'You couldn't make it up', but actually they did. Here in postmodernity 'facts' have become unimportant; spin is everything. Reality is therefore no longer divided, as by modernity, into facts and values, or truths of reason and truths of science. Reality is whatever you make of it. You make it up as you go along.

If reality is thus being merrily deconstructed, the same is even more true for stories. One of the best-known aspects of postmodernity is the so-called 'death of the metanarrative', the critique applied to the great stories by which our lives have been ruled. (Metanarratives are the big stories, or the big pictures: the big story of modernity is the myth of progress.) Again, you can see this clearly at the political level. The post-war generation lived by the myth that world politics consisted of the Cold War between East and West, and that once that got sorted out everything would be all right. When the USA basically won by default, Francis Fukuyama wrote a piece called 'The End of History?', suggesting that there was now nothing much more to happen.

But we still had, and have, the Middle East. We still have Northern Ireland. We still have the Balkans, Rwanda, the Sudan, and many other places that no longer make it into the newspapers (the selectivity of the media is another major feature of postmodernity) but that form running sores in our post-Cold-War world. And out of the Middle East has come yet more agony and shock, as the usual metaphor about 'waves of refugees' has become reality, bobbing around in the Mediterranean hoping desperately that someone will help. The big story about the 'end of history' was a lie. So too was the story that went with it, that fuelled all the excitement a few years ago about the so-called 'Arab Spring': the Western journalists and politicians imagined that 'history' was inexorably moving in the direction of getting rid of tyrants so that Western-style democracy would automatically spring up from the ground. That big story, too, was a lie, though the fact that the West believed it has contributed materially to the problems we all now face.

And when the big stories let us down, the little stories – the horrible, terrible human stories of a thousand atrocities – are still there, and we haven't a clue what to do about them. Precisely because postmodernity says 'my story matters', 'your story matters', 'everybody's story matters', so the people on each side in every conflict believe that their own story (usually told in terms of their being the victims) matters above all else. Actually, that isn't so very different from the origins of the First World War. The different European nations all had their local stories to tell, and from their points of view they were quite justified in going to war. So it goes to this day, in South Sudan, in Syria, in Northern Ireland . . . That is the political edge of post-modernity. The modernist myth we lived in was just a cover story. Now that that has been unmasked, our politicians haven't a clue what to do. One of the reasons is that very few of them have studied either philosophy or religious studies at university. They thought that wasn't practical enough. But what they are left with is mere short-term pragmatism.

Practical enough? I recall a wonderful moment in Oxford. A bright undergraduate who was studying theology spent his penultimate long vacation in Zambia working with local churches. He came back thrilled with what the churches were achieving in their local com-munities and more widely, and was all the more excited at the thought of theology supplying the tools to enable the church to be the church in what we used to call the 'third world'. He was determined to go back, as a trained theologian, and get stuck into development work. At the end of the next term, the head of the college where I was teaching, who had in his earlier life been an economic adviser to a Labour prime minister, asked this young man, 'What do you want to do?' Back came the answer, 'I'm going to be a development worker in the third world.' The provost looked puzzled. 'So why aren't you reading economics?' he asked. The student didn't miss a beat. 'Because theology is so much more relevant,' he replied.

He was right. The economist hasn't got any answers. The economy is like the engine of a car. The economists can tell you how it works and how to clean it and fix it. But they can't tell you which direction to drive the car.

The same is true, inevitably, with progress and Enlightenment themselves. Everybody's liberation turns out to be someone else's slavery. Everybody's economic boom turns out to be at someone else's expense. So, says postmodernity, all our great stories, our controlling narratives, are broken down into little stories: my story, your story, which may be 'authentic' in themselves; this really is how we feel things, how we see things. But they will almost certainly not impinge on one another. This is fine if we live in cyberspace, where we can create our own virtual realities, accessed from our suburban sitting rooms. But it makes no sense at all where there are real lines drawn on real pieces of ground, and human beings get shot if they cross them, or happen to be born the wrong side.

This break-up of large narratives into little ones, philosophically, again goes back to Nietzsche, who offered collections of aphorisms as the appropriate way of describing the world. Some novelists have experimented with this kind of thing. Famously, *The French Lieutenant's Woman* offered a choice of endings according to the reader's mood. Julian Barnes's *History of the World in Ten and a Half Chapters* offered no connected narrative at all, but only a succession of images, with, as he implied, the story like a raft adrift on an inhospitable ocean. It is interesting that in contemporary biblical studies some, not least those who have drunk deeply at the postmodern well, have preferred the hypothetical document 'Q' and the proto-gnostic document known as the *Gospel of Thomas* to the canonical gospels. They provide, after all, collections of detached sayings, rather than an overarching story. The same thing is seen culturally in the sudden rise in the UK, during the 1990s, of the radio station Classic FM, which offers snippets of music, only seldom indulging the older taste for complete symphonies, concerti and operas.

The bottom line of postmodernity is the deconstruction of the individual. No longer are we the masters of our fate, the captains of our soul. We are each a mass of floating signifiers, impulses and impressions. We are changing all the time. We reconstruct ourselves as we go along, according to the stimuli we receive, the spin that comes our way, the mood that, as we say, 'takes us'. The 'meaning' of a book, a poem, a work of art is not something inherent in the thing itself. It shifts according to the readers. Who is to say there is any objective meaning? If metanarratives are to be killed off, so are authors, whose intentions remain opaque behind the text. And – is there even a text, anyway?

Equally, you can see what happens if you transpose the same confusion into other spheres, such as politics, marriage and sexuality, or education. This is the postmodern dilemma: reality ain't what it used to be, the great stories have let us down, we aren't feeling ourselves any more. We are left with a pick-and-mix culture, an if-it-feels-good-do-it culture, a whatever-turns-you-on culture: the hippiedom of the 1960s come of age, all dressed up for the millennium but with nowhere to go. At the personal level, the culture is symbolized by the portable personal stereo, creating for its wearer a private and constantly shifting world of sound; or more darkly the pornography industry, now providing safe cyberspace or telephone sex for those who find real relationships with real human beings too complex or messy. At the corporate level, in the UK the Greenwich Dome was constructed as a classic postmodern project: a giant impressive space, which nobody knew what to do with. (It has since found various uses, but at the time it was a project in search of a purpose.) Despite its inventors' intentions, it was a near-perfect symbol of this confused, shifting, ambitious yet rootless culture.

Another even sharper example occurred at the widely televised funeral of the South African leader Nelson Mandela. As the speeches were being made, a man appeared on the platform and gestured wildly as though interpreting into sign language the speeches praising Mandela and his great achievements. But it became apparent that he was not, after all, a proper interpreter. His wild gestures meant nothing. One philosopher, however, commenting on this, declared that this man was the only one speaking the truth that day. The supposed transformation effected by Nelson Mandela's triumphant launching of the 'rainbow nation' a generation ago has still not worked its way through into the real lives of most of its inhabitants. The funeral became a classic postmodern moment. The person who seemed to be interpreting was in fact deconstructing.

The Bible within the postmodern world

What happens to the Bible within this culture I have so briefly described? I content myself with some notes on the way in which the postmodern climate has affected readings of the Bible. These, in good postmodern fashion, are random rather than systematic, but there is no space for the latter anyway.

Deconstructing the 'big story'

The first obvious thing is that the modernist critique of the Bible seems to be heightened. All great stories are suspect, so the Bible is not only politically incorrect because it told the wrong story (as the

Enlightenment thought) but it is under suspicion because it tells a story at all. Obviously, not all the biblical books are in narrative form. But the majority are. The present framing of the canon of scripture, and for that matter the various framings which the Jewish canon underwent, all emphasize an overarching narrative from a beginning to an end, with various sub-plots in between. This larger narrative, in one form or another, transcends, though it includes, the messages of the individual books.

If we take the Hebrew and Aramaic canon, leaving the New Testament out of the picture for a moment, we are left with reading either from Genesis to Malachi, or, in the way it is organized in the Hebrew Bible itself, from Genesis to 2 Chronicles. This is, manifestly, a story in search of an ending. The conclusion, whether of Malachi or 2 Chronicles, leaves one saying, 'Yes, and what next?' The Christian canon as we have it, factoring the New Testament back into the same picture, gives us that same story, with the four gospels saying, in their very different ways, 'This is the climax of the story', and then the epistles and the Apocalypse, saying 'Now this is what we do with it.' The book of Revelation ends with the wonderful image of the heavenly city coming down from heaven to earth, and this is not about 'going back to Eden'. Rather, it is the climax of the story which began with Genesis. It offers the glorious completion of the human project, God's project, the project of creation itself. That is the big story we find in the Christian canon.

Undeniably, there are some books that do not appear to provide a 'big story': books, for instance, like Proverbs or Ecclesiastes. But these not only hint at larger stories underneath the scattered maxims and wise sayings. They are held in their canonical contexts within a larger narrative framework of creation. They insist that 'wisdom', though relevant to all human life, is found and known supremely within the ongoing life, story and traditions of Israel.

But within postmodernity all such narrative settings are suspect. There are other stories, we are told, and these biblical ones may be oppressive. For example, the liberation theology of the 1960s built a great deal on the story of the exodus. That, we were told, was the paradigm for all the liberations the world now needed. Now, in postmodernity, people are pointing out that, if you simply tell the exodus story, you are left with a double problem: what are you going to say to the Egyptians at one end of the story, and the Canaanites at the other? We are reminded, for instance, that the Jewish way of tell-ing the narrative of the Middle East is now deeply damaging to the Palestinian communities who comprise most of the native Christians in that part of the world – and that the Palestinians and their sup-porters must be careful lest they tell *their* story in such a way as to eliminate the story of post-Holocaust Israel. And so on. We shouldn't be surprised that our politicians can't solve these problems. The stories we have lived in, under attack on all sides, have collapsed.

Deconstructing biblical reality

The biblical view of reality is also, naturally, under attack. Paul, we are told, saw things his way; but we should also bend over backwards to see things through the eyes of his opponents, who after all thought of themselves as Christians too, and may have had a point which Paul's rhetoric has masked from our sight. As we have often been told, it is the literature of the conqueror that survives. Graham Shaw's book *The Cost of Authority*, a polemic against Paul's supposed manipulation of his readers, is a classic postmodern protest against taking things at their face value. Shaw said, taking 2 Corinthians in particular, that Paul is not actually arguing passionately from the crucifixion of Jesus to a particular style of life. He is, instead, cynically manipulating his readers and hearers with rhetoric which sounds very impressive but is in fact just another power trip. That is a classic postmodern decon-struction of a book of the Bible.

The biblical view of the whole of reality, in which Jewish-style creational monotheism is by and large taken for granted, is also under attack. Some have argued that this rather one-dimensional and puri-tanical Deuteronomic viewpoint was imposed heavy-handedly upon various other viewpoints, scrunching the little stories of the cheerful and interesting semi-polytheists in Israel under the jackboot of a uniform, and subsequently canonized, monotheism. The imagery is not chosen at random. Memories, and imaginations, of the tyrannies of the first half of the twentieth century provide fertile soil for the protests of the second half. Postmodernism looks back to Hitler and Stalin and says, 'Modernism; that's what it always does.'

Deconstructing the biblical view of the person

The biblical view of the person, likewise, will not do for the relentless postmodernist. Who are you as a human being? The Jew and the

Christian both reply: 'I am made in the image of God.' The post-modernist asks, 'What could it mean to be made in the image of a god, when all god-stories are power-games?' Only that this, too, is a power-game, an example of 'speciesism' in which humans project a glorified version of themselves on to a hypothetical cosmic reality and use this to legitimate their oppression and rape of the rest of their world. Thus postmodern liberation theology, standing shakily on one part of the biblical narrative (the exodus tradition, shaky now because its own hidden motives have themselves been exposed, as we saw), critiques other parts of the Bible for their latent oppressive tendencies.

The hermeneutic which emerges from this kind of reading is itself very much characteristic of postmodernity's pick-and-mix, smorgasbord culture. You read the bits that resonate for you, you give them the spin that suits you, and then you use them to subvert the bits you don't like. (When you hear someone preaching in that way, that message carries no authority whatever. Allusions to the Bible within that framework are themselves in danger of being just power trips. If you can pick and mix, then all you are really saying is, 'I agree with the Bible wherever it agrees with me.')

The effect of all this is to set up a new version of the old idea of a 'canon within the canon'. In earlier versions of this procedure it might have been Luther's doctrine of justification calling the shots; now, it's Marx, Nietzsche and Freud. Obviously, no serious post-modernist would give any shelf-space to any doctrine of authority; if doctrines are themselves suspect, how much more something so dehumanizing, so tyrannical, as a doctrine of authority, not least the authority of a sacred text? Read this way, the Bible becomes one cultural artefact among many, to be drawn upon when useful and dumped when not. One might in the last analysis rely for guidance on Iris Murdoch, Dylan Thomas or François Lyotard. And many do.

The postmodern world

But supposing we are not satisfied by having our use of the Bible conditioned by the present cultural climate? Supposing we are not convinced by the postmodern claims themselves, and not happy with the proposal to trim down a lively and evidently fruitful Christian tradition on the Procrustean bed of postmodern theory?

There are several good reasons why we might be unconvinced, or, in postmodern style, simply unhappy with all this. For a start, there are the inner contradictions within postmodernism itself at the level of theory. To say 'all truth is relative' only works if the statement, that all truth is relative, is itself exempt from its own generalization. (All truths are relative, except the statement that all truths are relative!) Today's confused world is eager to deconstruct older moral ideals, but is equally eager to replace them with new ones. The person who is incensed if someone criticizes his or her alternative sexual lifestyle ('How intolerably medieval!') will be equally angry with the farmer in the UK who hunts foxes to protect his chickens, or the busy householder who fails to recycle bottles, cans and plastic bags. Even postmodernity's attack on all grand universal ideas becomes itself a grand universal idea. Its polemic against all metanarratives becomes itself a new metanarrative, a new Jack the Giant-killer in which the bold young underdog hero (postmodernism) slays boring old Giant Modernism. For all it deplores big stories, postmodernity too has one to tell. The death of the metanarrative is itself a metanarrative. The reason is not far to seek: postmodernity, too, is eschatological. It is a story about a history that is going somewhere; but the 'somewhere' towards which it is heading is chaos, cataclysm, meaninglessness. It is a secular version of the old *Götterdämmerung* epic, the 'Twilight of the Gods' as in Wagner's opera. We can't escape stories. Nor can we choose the endings we prefer.

There are interesting contradictions, too, lurking within the postmodern programme. The jazz musician Charlie Mingus once declared, 'In my music, I'm trying to play the truth of what I am. The reason it's difficult is because I'm changing all the time.' Notice that fascinating contradiction between two of the great postmodern agendas: the need to tell *my* story, rather than anyone else's – but, at the same time, the recognition that 'I', the 'self', is constantly in flux, deconstructed every moment. You can't imagine that troubling Bach, Mozart or even, dare I say, Louis Armstrong. The serious postmodernist would no doubt respond that that's precisely where we are at, and that anyone who wants consistency is asking for the moon. But are we bound to accept this verdict? Does the Bible, read for all it's worth and for all we're worth, have anything to say by way of reply? Yes it does.

In the Christian scriptures as we now have them we find, without much difficulty, a single overarching narrative. It is the story which runs from creation to new creation, from Eden to the New Jerusalem. This is the backdrop and ultimate context for everything else. The great bulk of the story, however, is focused quite narrowly on the fortunes of a single family in the Middle East, who are described as the chosen people through whom the creator God will act to rescue the whole world from its plight. The choice of this particular family does not imply that the creator has lost interest in other human beings, or in the cosmos at large. Quite the contrary. It is because he wishes to address them with his active and rescuing purposes that he has chosen this one family in the first place; his rescuing purposes are consistent with his overflowing generosity in creation itself. But the story of Israel, thus placed at the centre of the creator's plan for the world, contains a puzzle at its heart. The chosen people are themselves in need of rescue. (Think of a set of Russian dolls. Inside the creation story is the story of Israel; inside that again is the story of Jesus.) Even if we were to rearrange the books of the Old Testament, adopting (for instance) the normal Hebrew order in which the Prophets precede the Writings, so that Israel's scriptures end not with Malachi but with 2 Chronicles, we would still find ourselves reading a story in search of an ending. The people chosen to bring the creator's healing to the world are themselves in need of rescue and restoration.

The early Christian writings which came to be called the New Testament declare with one voice that this overarching story reached its goal in the life, death and resurrection of Jesus of Nazareth. The early Christians believed, on the basis of his public career and his resurrection, that he was Israel's Messiah, and that the divine intention not only *for* Israel but *through* Israel had been accomplished in him. In Jesus, in other words, the chosen people had found their rescue and restoration, though their self-appointed guardians and spokespersons had not seen it that way. (The first Christians picked up from Jesus himself the fact that this was nothing new: the ancient prophets had routinely warned that the people's official leaders were missing the point.) But if Jesus was and is Israel's Messiah, then another vital strand of ancient biblical hope comes into play. Israel's Messiah was always supposed to be the Lord of the whole world: this receives classic expression in some of the psalms (such as Psalm 2 or 72) and in the prophecies of Isaiah (for instance, chapters 11 and 42).

The idea that Jesus was the Lord of the world, that his message had worldwide significance, was not, then, a strange early Christian fantasy bolted on to Jesus but not really fitting with his own purpose and mission. It grows right out of first-century Jewish messianism itself. His followers then saw themselves as royal heralds, claiming the whole world for its new King. If in his resurrection he had defeated death itself, then the dark powers which held the world in thrall had been overcome, and all people could be set free from them to worship the one true God. If in his death he had taken on himself the weight of the world's sin, then the idea that 'Gentiles' (non-Jews) were automatically and for ever 'sinners' could be challenged. A new, healing power and life had burst upon the whole world.

That is why the early Christians saw themselves as living not simply in the *last* days – though there is a sense in which that is true as well – but in the *first* days, the beginning of the new creation that dawned when Jesus emerged from the tomb on Easter morning. They saw themselves, in other words, as living within a story in which the decisive event had already occurred and now needed to be implemented. Something had *happened* as a result of which the world was now a different place, even though not in the way they might have hoped or wanted. This is clear right across the New Testament. Even if we were to ignore Acts for the moment, this story of new creation is the implicit narrative which informs and undergirds all the epistles. The four canonical gospels, in their very different ways, are all only comprehensible if we understand them to be telling how the God-and-Israel story reached its goal in Jesus, and telling this story moreover from the perspective of those now charged with putting it into effect in and for all the world. Even if we were to rearrange the New Testament canon, this implicit story-line would still emerge at every point.

Notice what follows. There has been a fashion in recent decades for bringing back into the discussion of earliest Christianity various other documents, such as the so-called 'gospel of Thomas' or the sayings-source (usually called 'Q') which some scholars detect behind the material common to Matthew and Luke. But it is precisely in those documents, actual or reconstructed, that the sense of a story is lost. They are (to the delight of the postmodernist) aphoristic, gnomic, apparently random: not good *news* but only good *advice*. Jesus is then seen simply as a teacher of a strange and subversive wisdom, perhaps even of a religious 'gnosis' (a private knowledge, indeed a self-knowledge) in which the whole story of Israel and the creation is lost sight of in favour of a private religious experience or an individual protest against the ills of society. This is not to say, of course, that the New Testament does not offer 'religious experience' or social protest; only that these emerge from the narrative itself, rather than floating in a historical vacuum.

Once we grasp this point, we can see easily enough that the interface between the Bible and our own contemporary culture still bears a good deal of family likeness to the interface between early Christianity and its surrounding milieu. When we construe the Bible, in its own terms, as the true metanarrative, the strange history of the creator and the cosmos, the covenant God and the covenant people, the God who becomes human and dies for the sins of the world, the God who breathes his own breath into his followers and equips them to implement his victory in the world – when we read the Bible like this, we discover that this great metanarrative challenges and subverts several other worldviews. This can be puzzling or even threatening for Christians who learned the faith within the high modernism of the decades after the Second World War. Within that world, it was easy to imagine that the right way to 'use' the Bible to address the world was to abstract large chunky doctrines from the Bible and hurl them at the heads of people who believed large chunky modernist theory. But to do that you have to stop treating the Bible as what it is, namely, a story – the true story of the creator and the cosmos. Much better to let the Bible be what it is. Stories are far more subversive and damaging to other alternative worldviews than large abstract doctrines. In fact, when properly understood, 'doctrines' themselves are basically portable stories: they fold up narratives into shorthand phrases which enable us to discuss them, but to understand them properly you need to translate them back into stories again.

Challenges of the biblical metanarrative

Let me, then, sketch out five ways in which the biblical story works, laying foundations thereby for some of the points I want to make in my final section. This is, inevitably, only a summary of things which might be spelled out in much more detail.

To begin with, the biblical metanarrative challenges paganism, and our neo-pagan world. From creation to recreation, from the call of Abraham to the New Jerusalem which comes down from heaven to earth, the Bible presents itself as the truth of which paganism is the parody. Paganism sees the glory of creation, and worships creation instead of the creator. The grown-up version of this is pantheism, whether Stoicism in the ancient world or the varieties of New Age belief in the contemporary world. The mirror-image of this is dualism, the belief that creation is the work of a lesser god or indeed an anti-god. These alternatives – pantheism and dualism – feed off one another like the two sides in a long-running war of terrorist attrition. The pantheist can't deny the glory and power of creation. The dualist can't deny the horrible things that happen in the world. Each sees the folly of the other and so retreats into its own counter-affirmations.

One of the remarkable things about the Bible is the way in which, from Genesis to Revelation, these options are systematically rejected and undermined. There is one God, the creator; creation is good, but it is not God; the reality of evil in the world is not to be explained in terms of either an evil creation or an evil god, but is seen as an intrusion into the good creation, which is dealt with through the story of the chosen family. The world is God's world, 'charged with the grandeur of God', but also groaning as it awaits its rescue from corruption and decay.

This biblical challenge to paganism, and indeed to dualism, is huge and basic; I presuppose it in all that follows.

Second, the biblical metanarrative challenges and subverts the worldview of philosophical Idealism, in which historical events are mere contingent trivia, and reality is to be found in a set of abstractions, whether timeless truths or absolute values. Any attempt to see the biblical stories as simply illustrations of such timeless truths or absolute values is confronted by the biblical text itself, in which the opposite is the case: the love of God, the justice of God, the forgiveness of God, and so forth are invoked not to draw attention away from the historical sphere but to give it meaning and depth. The love of God, for example, is not just an abstract idea. It happened on the cross. The forgiveness of God is not just a nice theory. It happened when Jesus was hanging there with nails in his hands and feet, praying for his torturers. When the people of Israel invoked the justice of their God, what they wanted was to be liberated from their oppressive enemies. When the early Christians spoke of the love of God, they were referring to something that had happened in recent history, which had changed the way the real world actually was (not just *their* real world, we note, but *the* real world). That was, without a doubt, a bold claim. But if they were not making this claim, then they were, quite literally, talking nonsense.

This means, third, that the biblical metanarrative also challenges and subverts the non-storied aphoristic world both of the *Gospel of Thomas* (and similar documents) and of contemporary postmodernity. That is sharply relevant to contemporary debates about Jesus, not least with those who are most anxious in our own day to deconstruct what they see as the oppressive narrative and theology of the canonical gospels. They end up with a Jesus who functioned like a wandering Cynic, or perhaps a Gnostic, whose whole *raison-d'être* was to utter striking, paradoxical and challenging aphorisms, challenging the existing socio-cultural order but offering as an alternative merely a do-it-yourself way of constructing either one's inner religious world or one's relation to the outer world. As we saw a moment ago, this is the reflection, on the screen of supposed historiography, of the postmodern emphasis on deconstructing all metanarratives, and on the individual doing his or her own thing. In neither case, however, does this reconstructed Jesus belong within a story. In neither case does he announce the kingdom of God as a new fact bursting in upon the public world. Ironically, the attempt to deconstruct Jesus leaves one with a sort of secularized version of the private world of the dualistic pietist, in which Jesus and the Bible only tell me about myself, not about public reality.

The biblical metanarrative challenges all such attempts at deconstruction. It insists that there is a public world. It acknowledges that there are all sorts of problems in this public world, including the problem of knowledge itself (how can we be sure that we really do know what is 'out there'? Might we not be deceiving ourselves?). But instead of allowing these problems to dictate the terms of the debate, ending with deconstruction as the only apparent alternative to a brittle would-be 'certainty', the biblical metanarrative itself insists that the problems have been addressed and defeated by the creator himself. (This is not, please note, a Christian version of the modernist rejection of postmodernity. That is an ever-present temptation for some types of Christianity, and we should resist it.) The biblical metanarrative invites us to go through the postmodern critique of modernity, Christian modernity included, and out the other side into a new grasping of reality, a post-postmodernity.

Fourth, from the very beginning the biblical metanarrative challenged all pagan political power structures. This, indeed, is implicit in the very meaning of the word 'gospel'. In its Old Testament context, Isaiah spoke of the 'good news' that YHWH had overthrown the idols of Babylon, and thus had broken Babylon's grip on Israel. In its Greco-Roman context, 'gospel' referred to the good news of the birth or accession of an emperor. The New Testament, firmly rooted in the Jewish world of Isaiah and clearly addressing the Greco-Roman context, proclaimed the 'good news' that Jesus of Nazareth was the new, true emperor of the world, whose accession to supreme power was the healing, liberating, news for which the whole creation had been waiting. Here there is no middle ground. This proclamation was a statement either of public truth or of public falsehood. The one thing it could never be was a statement of a private truth, a statement of 'how I feel', a belief which involved the speaker's religious interiority but nothing else. The attempt to translate the gospel into such a thing is one of the great deceits of the modern period.

This emphasis on 'good news' about the real world was actually inherent in the original Jewish context. When Jesus spoke of the kingdom of God, he must have meant, within the Jewish world of his day, a reality which would challenge decisively the kingship of the existing authorities. That of course is part of the explanation, both historical and theological, of the crucifixion. When Paul spoke of the Lordship of Jesus, he was using for Jesus language which explicitly and obviously evoked the lordship of Caesar. There cannot be two Lords of the world.

From a Jewish point of view, the biblical metanarrative challenges all pagan power, deconstructing it in terms of its underlying idolatry and dehumanization. In its place, it offers the kingdom of God, as promise and hope. From the Christian point of view, the fuller biblical metanarrative makes the same challenge, but now with the sharp edge that on the cross (as Paul says in Colossians) the one true God has in Christ defeated all principalities and powers, leading them in his triumphal procession as a bedraggled, beaten bunch of has-beens. In their place is the one who says, in a way that postmodernity would never even dream of, 'All authority in heaven and on earth has been given to me.' Nor should we miss the point of who it is saying these things. Paul is in prison as he writes about the overthrow of the 'powers'. The Jesus who claims all authority is the one who has been crucified. These are not ways of claiming the ordinary kind of worldly power. They are affirming a different kind of power altogether.

Fifth: the biblical metanarrative – in which the story of God and the world develops, takes shape, and points to or reaches a climax – challenges all rival visions of the future ('eschatologies') and how we get there. This is so whether the biblical metanarrative in question is Jewish or Christian. Consider, for instance, the various political eschatologies which are advanced from time to time. Around the turn of the eras, the poets and historians at the court of the Roman emperor were telling the story of history in such a way as to indicate that it was reaching its climax with the new Roman 'Golden Age'. In the eighteenth and nineteenth centuries, many people began to tell the story of the development of Western democracy as though the establishment of one-man-one-vote, and then one-person-one-vote, or even dare I say it, proportional representation, was going to usher in the new Golden Age.

At the time of preparing this book for publication, a new movie is celebrating the work of the Suffragette movement in the early twentieth century. It now seems incredible to us that women were denied the vote for so long; but it is also clear that this great democratic movement has not brought about a secular Utopia. Part of the reason for the deep cynicism of Tacitus, Juvenal and others at the end of the first century, and for the deep cynicism of many commentators at the end of the twentieth, was and is that the Golden Ages have let us down. We pressed all the buttons and the toy didn't work. That was the point about the outpouring of grief after the death of Princess Diana. People said Diana was a modern princess; but she wasn't, she was a *post*modern princess. She had lived in the 'great dream'. She had found her Prince Charming. She had everything going for her; and the dreams let her down. That's why in Western culture she was an icon of where we are in postmodernity. And that is why her image lives on in the hearts of many who had themselves lived the romantic modernist dream and woken up to face ordinary reality.

Consider, also, the great eschatological claim represented both by the words 'Renaissance' and 'Enlightenment'. Whoever invented the idea of the Middle Ages was, in retrospect, one of the most powerful people in Western history. Whoever invented the idea that humankind had 'come of age' in the eighteenth century was equally powerful, if not more so. (People didn't sit there during the Middle Ages saying, 'It's a bit boring in the Middle Ages; I wonder when they are going to end.' It was a later invention by someone telling a three-stage story in order to legitimate and celebrate a world of innovation.) So too with 'Enlightenment'. Before the Enlightenment people didn't sit around saying, 'It is rather dark, isn't it?' The Enlightenment did not claim to be a return to a previous cultural golden age. Science, technology, modern democracy – all this was new. All history was to be seen as leading up to this great climax of technological advance, historical and theological scepticism, political revolution and so forth, which were then to be implemented to dispel the long night of pre-Enlightenment superstition and slavery. This story, then, has merely two stages: first the dark, now the light. But the label is, equally, a cultural power-play.

The ideas of 'Renaissance' and 'Enlightenment' are actually rival eschatologies to Christianity. They are telling a story of world history and development with the climax somewhere else other than Jesus. Christianity tells a story about the world reaching its climax in Jesus of Nazareth. They do it differently.

No-one can deny that the Christian story is hard to believe. The world is still full of murder and mayhem. We still face disaster and death on a large scale. But that isn't the point – as the early Christians had to reassure one another. Something *has* changed. Jesus *has* been raised from the dead and the new creation has begun – and the Spirit *has* been poured out so that real transformation is possible, for human beings and for the wider society and world. And after all, the grandiose claims of the 'Renaissance' and the 'Enlightenment' are themselves full of holes; and as they are shown up, so the true point of the gospel shines out all the more brightly. We live in a world where, increasingly, people are clutching at straws, unable to glimpse a story which would lead the way into true peace, freedom and justice. The Christian gospel offers such a story. But to tell it truly, you have to be living it. It is up to those who read the Bible and take it seriously to set about living by its eschatological message of new creation and so forming the community that cannot be decon-structed, because it is a community of love. That is the real challenge to the church as it seeks to be faithful in witnessing to the God whose world this is.

A biblical challenge to postmodernity

Let us then take the three elements of postmodernity and suggest what a reading of the Bible might have to say at each point.

A biblical metanarrative of love.   I have already stressed that the Bible as a whole, as well as in most of its parts, presents us with a large, overarching narrative. Postmodernity is bound to object: metanarratives are controlling, dominating, and we all know the ways in which this story too has been used politically, socially and personally to bolster this or that power trip. But the biblical metanarrative itself resists being abused in this fashion, because it is the story of love. The biblical metanarrative offers itself as the one story which cannot be deconstructed, to which the criticisms of Marx, Nietzsche and Freud are not relevant. (Look at Jesus on the cross: was he doing that for money? Was he doing it for power? Was he doing it for sex? Of course not. It was an act of love.) The story speaks from first to last of a God who did not need to create, but who did so out of overflowing and generous love. It speaks of a God who did not need to redeem and recreate, but did so as the greatest possible act of self-giving love.

The problem is, however, that our telling of this story, and our living of the story as Christians, not least as modernist Western Christians, has often been a power-play of our own. This problem is all the more acute for those of us who have lived and worked within an established church. But the biblical metanarrative itself is not a controlling narrative: it is a self-giving narrative. If it is to make sense, those who read it and are formed by it are called to become a self-giving community. The Achilles heel of postmodernity is the fact that it cannot recognize love, but insists on deconstructing it.

If, then, we are to address contemporary culture with the message of the Bible, we must get used to combining two things which are normally at opposite poles: humility and truthtelling. For us, an intellectual humility has come to mean saying something like, 'I would want to argue x, y or z': in other words, I wouldn't go so far as actually to assert this, because that might offend you. My opinions are only my opinions and they might be wrong. Truthtelling has come to appear as arrogance ('There are two ways of looking at things: the right way, and your way'). Somehow we have to tell the truth, but to tell it as the liberating story, the healing story, the true story.

And the best way we can do this is by telling, again and again, in story and symbol and acted drama, the biblical story, focused on the story of Jesus himself, the true story of the Word made Flesh. That is why the great symbol at the heart of Christianity is the symbol of the Eucharist. It re-enacts the whole story and offers it as food for hungry hearts and lives.

Biblical promises for the deconstructed self. If we are telling and living the true story, we will discover, within it, that it contains promises for deconstructed selves. We Christians shouldn't actually be afraid of deconstruction. It points in its own way to the truth that Jews, Christians and many others regularly acknowledge, that all our righteousness is as filthy rags. Clearly, if we are arrogant modernist individuals (captains of our fate, and masters of our soul) we need to die with Christ. If deconstruction is a rather oblique way of pointing us to that, so be it. But what postmodernism never notices is that after death comes resurrection. The truth of baptism is precisely the truth of new life the other side of death. Here we need, I believe, to develop – as an essential part of the engagement between the Bible and contemporary culture! – a better and richer theology of worship, the worship of the true and living God. It is through worship that we are renewed in the image and likeness of God, coming up the other side after deconstruction like a baptized person emerging from the water. It is easy for the church to slide back into some version of the Enlightenment dream, so that a Christian, and particularly a church leader, can think of herself or himself as an isolated, lonely individual. The church is called to be the community of resurrected selves: persons undergoing reconstruction; and that reconstruction itself only happens within the community of the Body of Christ.

A biblical way of knowing. In this life, we can and must think in terms of reconstituted reality and genuine knowing. Yes, we must take on board the full postmodern critique of those arrogant Enlightenment epistemologies (theories of knowledge) in which a supposed objectivism was actually a cloak for political and social power and control. The empires of the eighteenth and nineteenth centuries made their way on the back of their new technologies: they used their 'objective' discoveries as a way of taking over the world and using it for their own ends. Powerful rulers have always decided what would count as 'truth' and have used sheer force to make actual reality conform to it. But when all is said and done, it is part of the true human task, given in Genesis and reaffirmed in Christ, that we should know God, and one another, and the world, not with a spurious hard 'objectivity' as if we were flies on the wall, but with a genuinely human knowledge. Paul speaks of being 'renewed in knowledge after the image of the creator'. This knowledge is always *relational*, but that doesn't mean it is merely *relativized*.

This means that we need to work towards a better understanding of 'knowledge' itself. The normal accounts of 'knowing' which underlie today's popular discourse collapse into those two spurious alternatives, a supposed 'objectivity' and the relativized 'subjectivity'. In modernity, the former is given precedence: would-be-objective scientific knowing: test-tube epistemology, if you like. Every step away from this is seen as a step into obscurity, fuzziness and subjectivism, reaching its nadir in metaphysics. Instead, I believe that a biblical account of 'knowing' should follow philosophers such as Bernard Lonergan, a great Catholic philosopher of the last generation, and take *love* as the basic mode of knowing. Genuine human knowing might be seen as variations on the theme of love, with the love of God as the highest and fullest sort of knowing that there is. All other forms of knowing might be seen as derived from that.

The point about love is that, when I love, I affirm and celebrate the differentness of the beloved. Not to do that is not to love at all, but to lust. (Not for nothing is pornography one of the dark and powerful symbols of the postmodern world.) But, at the same time, when I truly love I am not a detached observer, the fly-on-the-wall of objectivist epistemology. I am passionately and compassionately involved with the life and being of the beloved, whether this is an object, a piece of music, a person or ultimately God himself. But though I am thus fully involved, caught up in the process of knowing – in other words, with my 'subjectivity' fully engaged – this does not mean that there is nothing which is being known. Or, to put the same point the other way round, though I am really 'knowing' a reality which is other than, and outside, my own mind and imagination, this does not mean I am a detached, uninvolved observer. Of course, within the hard sciences, the *appropriate* form of 'knowing' is one in which the human element in observation is reduced as far as possible; but it is still humans who set up the experiment, and from Heisenberg onwards we have learned that even the act of observation changes, in mysterious ways, the reality of what is being observed. Anyway, I believe we can and must give an account of human knowing for the post-postmodern world which will amount to what we might call an epistemology of love.

This can and should emerge from a fresh engagement with the biblical narrative of what it means to be truth-telling humans within God's world. This is part of what it means to be genuinely human, to be image-bearers. As the 'royal priesthood', those who belong to Jesus, rescued by his death from all forms of death including decon-struction itself, we are on the one hand to speak truth into the world so that God's reality may be known, and on the other hand to speak the true praises of the world back to its creator.

Living out the story

I have here attempted to give – in very brief and shrunken form! – an account of narrative, selfhood and knowing which embodies and reflects the biblical metanarrative itself. I have suggested, in other words, that it is our task not just to tell but to live out the story; that the model of God's self-giving love in creation, covenant, judgment, mercy, incarnation, atonement, resurrection, wind and fire, and ultimately recreation must be the basis for our self-understanding, our life and our vocation. When we do this, we discover, I believe, that the reality of which we are dimly aware (but which our ontol-ogies, whether pre-modern, modern or postmodern, find slipping through their fingers) is best described in the biblical language of heaven and earth, created, sustained, redeemed and to be renewed by the living God known in Jesus and in the Spirit. The Bible does not, then, tell us to ignore postmodernity and to carry on as though modernity were still what mattered. Far from it. The Bible tells a story which will lead us through postmodernity's necessary critique of modernity and on, through and out the other side. And all this leads me, finally, to what is perhaps the most important point of all.

We live at a moment of extraordinary opportunity. The worlds of today and tomorrow offer a remarkable challenge for serious and joyful Christian mission to post-postmodern society. Some people seem to yearn for the days when things were nice and simple, when a supposedly 'biblical' gospel of 'salvation from sin and going to heaven' could be preached to people who were, in effect, unsuccessful

Pelagians, trying to pull themselves up by their moral bootstraps. But we can't go back to the 1950s. (Someone said of the church that it is now finally and gloriously ready for the 1950s! What an indictment: we have got to be getting ready for 2025 and 2040, and teaching our young people how to engage with the newest issues, not preaching to the worlds we grew up in.) Nor, however, can we or should we succumb to postmodernity itself, though it may well be that for some people and groups a time of penitence, in which modernist nonsense can be purged and rethinking can begin, might be a good idea.

We live, as I have said, at a time of cultural crisis. At the moment I don't hear too many people pointing a way forward out of the postmodern morass. Some people are still trying to put up the shutters and live in a pre-modern world. Many are clinging to modernism for all they can. Many are deciding that living off the pickings of the garbage-heap of postmodernity is the best they can do. It isn't simply that the Bible, and the Christian gospel, offers us a religious option which can outdo other religious options, can fill more effectively the slot labelled 'religion' on the cultural and social smorgasbord. It is, rather, that the Bible and the Christian gospel point us, and indeed urge us, to be at the leading edge of the whole culture, articulating in story and music and art and philosophy and education and poetry and politics and theology, and even academic biblical studies, a worldview which will mount the historically rooted Christian challenge to both modernity and postmodernity, leading the way into the post-postmodern world with joy, humour and gentleness, with good judgment and true wisdom.

3

Pilate, Caesar and Bible truth

I have spent most of my adult life trying to hold the Bible and the contemporary world together. I have tried to discern the ways in which what most Christian churches call 'the authority of the Bible' actually impinges on the real world, rather than merely on the private reality, or even the virtual reality, of a Christian existence which has detached itself from that world. Conversely, I have tried to discern ways in which the questions of our own day, framed in their own terms, can be brought to the Bible in the hope of finding, if not exact and complete answers, at least wisdom by which to take matters forward.

Whenever I think of this challenge, my mind goes to one of the most remarkable of the conversations which Jesus has with an individual in John's gospel, that final and fateful dialogue with Pontius Pilate in John chapters 18 and 19. I want to suggest here that this conversation contains within it the key elements of several of our most urgent and thorny current public debates, and that reflecting on it in the light of them, and them in the light of it, may help us both to understand John's gospel better and to address our contemporary issues with a more biblically grounded Christian comment. I shall then offer some concluding reflections on the sort of exercise I have been undertaking, not for the sake of navel-gazing but because some remarks on method, in the light of some actual practice, may be of interest or even of value to those who want to take things further.

First, a few words of introduction about John's gospel, and this discourse as part of it; then about the questions we face in our contemporary world.

Jesus and Pilate in John 18—19: introduction

John's gospel, as many people know, is different – different from Matthew, Mark and Luke, but also different in tone and mood from the other great theologian of the New Testament, namely Paul. Some who are temperamentally attracted to Paul are repelled by John, and vice versa. I have come to hope that it may be a mark of maturity that, after decades of studying Paul and the synoptic gospels, I have arrived late at a fascination with John. That fascination has not yet had time to take in much recent scholarship, as may be apparent to any specialists reading this. However, it may nevertheless be worth drawing attention to three things that strike me as specially important for this chapter.

First, the extended conversation between Jesus and Pilate comes within a long line of such one-on-one Johannine conversations. Jesus has engaged in conversation with many others, from Nicodemus in chapter 3 and the Samaritan woman in chapter 4, right through to this point. In the last two chapters of the gospel, there are three further brief but explosive conversations, with Mary at the tomb, with Thomas in the upper room and then finally with Peter by the lake. This sort of conversation simply doesn't happen in the synoptic gospels, where we tend to get either longer discourses (such as the Sermon on the Mount) or the one-liners with which Jesus answers an interlocutor, or comments on something that has just happened. And my impression is that those who have studied and preached on John and have drawn attention to these other conversations have not always taken so seriously this one with Pontius Pilate. Elsewhere, after all, Jesus can be presented as engaging with people with a view to bringing them to faith, or to stirring up a greater faith. Such conversations can then be used as models for personal evangelism or pastoral work. One might just about suggest that this is present, too, in the conversation with Pilate, but that doesn't seem to be the main point. Rather, what seems to be going on is the bringing together of the word of God with the words of the world. The specific conversations between Jesus and these various individuals, powerful though they are as personal encounters and therefore helpful in preaching and teaching, are also signs and symptoms of something much larger. That larger reality is flagged up in John's Prologue: he was in the world, the world was made by him, but the world didn't know him. He came to his own, and his own didn't receive him. But to all who received him, who believed in his name, he gave the right to be called God's children.

These Johannine conversations are designedly *representative*, drawing together the quintessence of Jesus' challenge, and hence God's challenge through his incarnate Word, both to his own people of Israel and to the larger world. And here at last, climactically, we shouldn't be surprised that we find a sharp extended conversation between Jesus, representing and embodying the living word of the creator God to his world, and Pontius Pilate, representing obviously the kingdom of Caesar, widely and rightly regarded at the time as the climactic and quintessential pagan world empire. There is thus a sense in which all the other conversations are focused in this one. It isn't so much that this is the odd one out, but rather that in this one the basic challenge of the word of God to the world as it is can be seen at its starkest. Perhaps – though this is not my theme in this chapter or indeed this book – we ought to re-read and re-preach those other conversations, not simply as pastoral and evangelistic challenges in the old way, but as the pastoral and evangelistic outworkings of this kingdom-challenge, the ultimate confrontation which is at last revealed.

That leads to the second introductory point about St John's gospel and about this conversation within it. One of the main questions Christians have asked down the centuries concerns the meaning of Jesus' death. We all know he died for our sins, but we all have different ways of saying what exactly that means. Traditionally, when this question has been applied to the gospels it has precipitated a search for particular clues, sending us to the various models of atonement theology: representative, substitute, exemplar, cosmic victory and so forth. But John doesn't appear to give us much help with this. (Actually, when approached in this way, neither do Matthew, Mark or Luke.) Even the famous final cry from the cross, *tetelestai*, 'It is finished' (John 19.30), is not primarily designed to make the point many preachers have found in it, that of a final account being settled or paid ('It's done!'). The original echo is older and more centrally biblical: we are meant to hear the statement in Genesis, that at the end of the sixth day God 'finished' all the work that he had begun. If we come to the gospels looking for the meaning of Jesus' death, then what all four gospels do, with John here in the lead, is to address the question by means of their various accounts of the trials, or hearings, to which Jesus was subject. These are not simply the historical appendage of 'what actually happened', leaving the question of theological meaning to a different level altogether. They are themselves the explanation of the meaning.

It is after all vital for John that in hearing the story of Jesus we are discovering what it meant that the Word became flesh and dwelt, pitched his tent, in our midst. If John is explaining the meaning of Jesus' crucifixion, he is doing so, not by adding extra bits of atonement theology to the conversation with Pilate but by highlighting the main themes of that conversation itself. The discourse before us in chapters 18 and 19 concerns the charges against Jesus, the nature of his kingdom if any, the question of truth, and the wrangle about power, and especially imperial power. All this, for John, is not something *other than* the meaning of the cross – and vice versa. One of the most disturbing phenomena about the interchange between the Bible and the contemporary world, I shall suggest, is that when we bring together our various worlds we find that even our most cherished doctrines may look different, may have more dimensions than we had imagined. Indeed, the tasks of systematic theology themselves may look different, though that is clearly a topic we cannot pursue here. By this I certainly do not mean, as an older liberal theology was perhaps too eager to say, that when we bring the Bible and the world together, or indeed when we approach Christian theology in the light of newer biblical criticism, we find we have to give up cherished formulations. Rather, I believe, we find those formulations brought up in three dimensions, casting both new light and new shadows in perhaps unfamiliar ways. Thus my second point about Jesus and Pilate in John 18 and 19 is the observation that this conversation cannot simply be a detached discourse about politics and philosophy. It draws those topics into the question of the meaning of the death which Jesus is about to suffer.

This leads directly to my third initial observation about the conversation between Jesus and Pilate. It picks up and draws together various important threads from earlier in the gospel which it is all too easy for the ordinary contemporary Western reader to ignore. Throughout the second half of the gospel, in fact, there has been a crescendo of important hints about what Jesus is going to accomplish when he gets to Jerusalem. Unless we see the conversation with Pilate as the place where they reach their climax, we will understand neither them nor it. I simply trace them here without further comment.

In chapter 12, on arriving in Jerusalem, Jesus receives a request from some Greeks that they should see him (12.21). Rather than respond directly, he comments that 'the hour has come for the Son of Man to be glorified', and continues with the saying about a grain of wheat falling into the earth and dying so that it may bear much fruit. Jesus then, troubled in spirit, prays that the Father would glorify his name, and a voice comes from heaven, 'I have glorified it, and will glorify it again.' Jesus comments that the voice has come for the crowd's sake, because 'Now is the judgment of this world; now the ruler of this world will be driven out. And I, when I am lifted up from the earth, will draw all people to myself' (12.31–32). In case we miss the point, John comments that Jesus said this to indicate the kind of death he would die. It is sometimes pointed out that the saying about drawing all people to himself appears to be the somewhat long-range answer to the question from the Greeks, eleven verses earlier. But it is quite a new thought in the gospel, and one for which many contemporary readers are quite unprepared, that central to the Johannine meaning of Jesus' death might be the idea of judging the world and driving out its present ruler so that those who are presently under that alien rule can be embraced by the creator, the God of Israel. Only in this light, however, I suggest, can we understand what is actually going on throughout John 18 and 19, not least the way in which Jesus appears to take charge, though in a way hitherto unprecedented. Jesus appears to be saying that the citizens of the wider world are at present under the rulership of a usurper, but that when he is 'lifted up' that rule will be broken and his own saving and healing rule will take its place.

Two passages in the 'Farewell Discourses' (John 13—17) bear this out. They, too, are often ignored but are in fact a key – one among many – to the deeper meaning. In chapter 14, Jesus speaks of his imminent 'going away', and the chapter ends (verses 30 and 31) with him declaring that 'the ruler of this world is coming'. 'He has no power over me,' Jesus comments, 'but I do as the Father has commanded, so that the world may know that I love the Father.' Here it is becoming clear. 'The ruler of this world' is the dark power which embodies itself in this or that particular human authority structure. The greatest of those structures – the high priesthood of the Jews on the one hand, the representative of Caesar on the other – are going to get together to do something to Jesus which they would not be able to do were it not the Father's will. We already know from the opening of chapter 13 that this is ultimately the work of 'the satan', the 'accuser', using Judas to 'accuse' Jesus to the authorities. But John does not seem to distinguish sharply between the human forces of wickedness and the dark non-human powers that operate through them.

This then points ahead to the extraordinary and dense passage in chapter 16, in which Jesus describes the future work of the Spirit: 'When [the Spirit] comes,' he says in verses 8–11, 'he will convict the world of sin and righteousness and judgment: of sin, because they do not believe in me; of righteousness, because I go to the Father, and you see me no more; of judgment, because the ruler of this world has been judged.' I shall return later on to this passage, because it is important for working out how the church in the power of the Spirit is meant to carry forward the achievement of Jesus. For the moment I simply note that Jesus speaks of the judgment, or condemnation, of 'the ruler of this world' as, effectively, a past event. It has happened. That is why, at the end of chapter 16, in verse 33, he can declare: 'In the world you face persecution. But take courage; I have conquered the world!' From the exhilarating perspective of Jesus' fellowship with his disciples on that last night, everything appears to have been accomplished already. The world's ruler has been judged and condemned; the world itself has been conquered. Somehow, the fate which is about to befall Jesus must bear this meaning. Nor is this to be an incidental by-product, a kind of political 'extra' sitting uncomfortably beside a normal sin-and-salvation atonement theology. It is, for John, part of the core meaning of Jesus' imminent death. This, I suggest, is the sequence of thought which then bursts into full flower in the conversation with Pilate.

This is, then, a *representative* conversation; a conversation *which gives meaning to Jesus' death*; and a conversation which draws out and displays more fully the earlier hints about *Jesus' victory over the ruler of this world*, a victory through which he himself will be installed as the rightful ruler who will draw to himself the peoples who up to now have been subject to this other, usurping ruler. I now turn to some introductory words on what might seem a totally different subject, namely some of the challenges that face us in our contemporary world. I shall then do my best to bring the two together.

Contemporary world: introduction

From time to time I have enjoyed brainstorming with groups of students and clergy on the key issues that face us in today's world.

The range of topics is bewildering. War, including nuclear war; global warming and the care of the environment; poverty and hunger; natural disasters; economic crises and strategies, not least international debt (which I have often highlighted as the major moral issue of our day); the failure of the secularization thesis in our increasingly obviously highly religious world, and the shrill reaction to that failure from some who regard all religion as a dangerous delusion. Many of these issues come together rather obviously in the present disastrous situation in the Middle East and the refugee crisis which is the ongoing and terrible result (not to mention the crisis in the Western nations which have no idea what to do about it). Then there are other continuing crisis-points: about gender roles and behaviour, about cultural and ethnic diversity and the question of what can and cannot be embraced within a plural society; about medical ethics, particularly concerning the beginnings and endings of human life. There are questions of crime and punishment, of education and literacy, of the impact of information technology on every aspect of human life, of the role and regulation of the media, and so on, and so on. In and behind it all, often unnoticed but massive, there is the crisis of global politics: the present American empire and the question of the next superpowers, China and/or India, the important but weak United Nations, and – let's call a spade a spade – the crisis of Western democracy itself, which could be summarized by saying that we can all now vote but we've all forgotten why. The present British muddles about possible constitutional reform, including the possible partition of the United Kingdom and the possible detachment from the European Union, reflect the multiple uncertainties in our society as to what political power is and what it's for. To imagine, as some seem to do, that Western democracy is the perfect political system, and that if only everyone else adopted it Utopia would finally arrive, looks like a bit of displacement activity, designed to distract attention from the fact that we've had this democracy for two centuries and many of our problems are just as intractable as they were before.

The signs are not good. In the diocese I was privileged to serve as Bishop, there are still schools where the teachers cobble together some cash to buy shoes for the children so that they can attend, while a Labour government, faced with massive fraud in the banking system, cobbled together a few billion pounds to enable the very rich to go on paying themselves enormous bonuses. In the aftermath of

September 11, 2001, the then Prime Minister, Tony Blair, who was MP for one of the constituencies in my diocese, declared that he was going to solve the problem of evil both in the Middle East and in Africa. But he couldn't even solve it in the part of the country he was representing in Parliament.

All of those issues would constitute enough topics for several books, and I am not competent to pronounce in detail on very many of them. I want simply to highlight three contemporary flashpoints of interest which draw together some of these themes, and to place them within a larger trio of issues which will enable us to ask how on earth a book like John's gospel might have something to say to a world like ours.

First, consider the still puzzling place of religion in our society. Religion is frequently in the news, even if often for the wrong reasons. When Pope Benedict XVI visited the UK in 2010, the media focused attention on several issues in which, for want of serious analysis, our secular world relies on gut reaction. There was of course a crisis of revelations about sexual abuse within the church. It was and is right to highlight that as a major failure and scandal, and to put in place better means of preventing such a thing happening again. But that issue was not the heart of why the papal visit caused such a stir. (One cannot escape the impression that the reason the media concentrated on sex had as much to do with prurience, and with a desire to thumb one's nose at the church that preached chastity but didn't live it.) Western society can't get its collective head around the fact that the Pope is both a religious leader and a head of state. (The Queen, too, is officially both; obviously the parallel is, for historical reasons, not accidental.) And just as the secular press can't understand the church–state situation, so they can't understand either why millions of people still take Christianity itself very seriously. Actually, though it used to be fashionable to speak of our increasingly secular society, the rumour of angels hasn't gone away – even though many who hunger for 'spirituality', or who experience it in some form or other, now assume that it isn't what the church is about. And the attempts of the commentators to highlight continuing divisions in the church don't get to the heart of what's going on, either. Despite some surface noise, there has been considerable rapprochement over the last decades between almost all Christian denominations, so that for many of us non-Romans the Pope came to the UK as the leader, not of a dangerous alternative religion, but of a sister church, with whom we still have serious differences but with whom, we increasingly realize, we share far more than we used to think. The papal visit, then, raised questions not only of the truth-claims of Christians in general and Roman Catholics in particular, but of the place of 'religion' in today's Western world, and of the possibility that a visitor from outside might point out to us that the UK has become, if it was not *de facto* already, a world centre of atheism as well as some very lively Christianity. Things are more complicated – and interesting – than people often suppose.

The second feature of our contemporary world I want to highlight is the odd and I believe dangerous mixture of pragmatism and idealism that passes for political philosophy among our elected politicians. Tony Blair's autobiography produced predictable comments; one point I haven't seen made, but which I think should be, is that for someone who made no secret of his own Christian faith, and latterly Catholic faith, there is nothing I can see in his book, and certainly nothing in the Index, to indicate any mention of or interaction with any bishops, archbishops, cardinals or other religious leaders. It seems as if the famous phrase of his chief spin-doctor, Alastair Campbell, that 'Downing Street doesn't do God', really went all the way to the top. The massive assumed disjunction between religious faith and public life, which has been the staple of post-Deist European and particularly American society for two hundred years, continued unabated both in the shiny idealism of Blair himself and in the less shiny but still idealistic approach of his successor. (I have to say that one of the finest speeches I have ever heard from a politician was that by Gordon Brown during the 2008 Lambeth Conference, on the ending of poverty; sadly, little happened as a result.) At the time of going to press (late 2015) one is struck more by opportunism than idealism; once the big narratives have gone, that is all that's left.

With Tony Blair, of course, there was a serious knock-on problem, which still exists. If a Christian politician doesn't think through a serious Christian political theology, his (or her) private faith may encourage him to think that he is the person to stand in the breach, to overthrow evil, to cast out the ruler of this world. Secularism cannot prevent, but rather enhances, the messianic temptation. And naturally the militant atheist will think in exactly the same way, with the secularist creed substituting for the sacred one and with, again, him- or herself as the secular messiah. But at no point do I detect a serious engagement with questions of what democracy ought to be and how it ought to work; still less any thought that Christian faith, which many leading politicians still profess, has anything particular to say on this subject. As a result, all the ancillary debates (which in the UK would include questions about having bishops in the House of Lords) are framed in what, to my mind, is the wrong context.

This continuing separation of religion from public life has not, evidently, been easy to maintain. Several times recently magazines you might have thought would never touch God with a bargepole have devoted cover stories to the questions raised by issues like the banning of Muslim headscarves or indeed Christian crosses. It has become clear that many in our society know there's a tricky issue there but don't know what to do about it. Some paint a caricature of totalitarian theocracy as a way of frightening people into leaving God out of the equation. Many, including alas many Christians, have no idea that Christianity has anything interestingly different to say on the relevant topics.

Among the caricaturists we find the third flashpoint, the continuing and shrill anti-God protests of Richard Dawkins and similar writers. Richard Dawkins is typical of someone who insists on yesterday's analysis, and yesterday's solution, for tomorrow's problem. Just as politicians regularly try to fit all issues into the questions and agendas of a generation ago (when many of them were eager young activists), so the high priests of secular scientism (as opposed to real science) are trying to have one last heave and get God off the map once and for all. These are classic cases of someone with a hammer assuming that all problems basically require nails.

What we are seeing, politically and in secular scientism, is a set of essentially *modernist* responses to aspects of an essentially *postmodern* world – just as the Bush–Blair coalition produced a classic modernist response, namely lots of bombs and tanks, to a classic postmodern problem, the rise of global terrorism. As I shall suggest in a minute, part of our problem is that just as the left–right politics of a former generation doesn't fit today's confused society, and just as the 'let's go and bomb them' geopolitics doesn't fit today's dangerous world, so the 'let's get rid of God' philosophy of Dawkins, and the much cooler suggestion of Stephen Hawking that the final 'gap' for God may have disappeared, simply don't fit the question. As many have pointed out, Stephen Hawking was still assuming an eighteenth-century god-of-the-gaps theology which no serious Christian or Jew would propose. But the public discussion of such issues shows, I think, that as a society we still lapse back to conceiving of problems in their eighteenth-century guise, whether it be left–right politics or god-of-the-gaps science-versus-religion stand-off – or, indeed, gunship diplomacy. All the philosophy of the last two centuries and we still can't break out of the public mindset that preceded them. In the middle of it all, many if not most Western Christians still assume that their faith has little or nothing to say to such politics, such worldview-crises or such global behaviour.

I shall shortly suggest that John's gospel, and indeed the rest of the New Testament, is eager to tell us a different story. But let me briefly locate these three contemporary flashpoints, and the welter of other issues I mentioned earlier, on the map of three larger concerns about which I have written and spoken elsewhere. Three of the big issues which shape our public life today, I have suggested, are Gnosticism, empire and postmodernity, which are toxic enough in themselves but particularly deadly in combination. (On all this, see, again, *Creation, Power and Truth* (London: SPCK, 2013).) Gnosticism declares that the world of space, time and matter is trivial or irrelevant; that human beings (or at least some of them) have a divine spark within them which needs to be discerned and lived out; that for this you need, not the death and resurrection of Jesus, but rather illumination or enlightenment which you might get from him or indeed from somewhere or someone else; and that, when this enlightenment has come, it will lead you not to the world of politics, of working for justice and peace, but to the cultivation of your own spirituality. Many, including many Christians, have eagerly embraced something like this. Indeed, though the Western Enlightenment has brought great blessings to the world, it has also encouraged forms of Gnosticism which are all the more powerful for being usually unrecognized.

Gnosticism flourishes, historically, in a world where empires control the lives of so many that outward change seems unimaginable. By the same token, empires encourage Gnosticism, because, whereas someone who declares that 'Jesus is Lord' may draw the conclusion that Caesar is not, someone who says 'Jesus has shown me that I am a spark of light needing to be set free from a wicked world' is unlikely to cause much trouble. Today's global empire is of a different sort from earlier ones, since the iron grip of the USA (and not least its financial institutions) is imposed on the world not through political organization – indeed, if that were the case, local groups might have a chance to vote for their actual rulers, which at present they do not – but through economic pressures, and the accident of the West being the 'last man standing' at the end of the Cold War. But, as many have pointed out, the 'novus ordo saeclorum' announced on every US dollar bill was and remains a powerful evocation of Virgil's hailing of the empire of Augustus as a 'new order of the ages'. The ideology of the Enlightenment thus reinforces the apparently effortless superiority of the West, with all the malign consequences (as well as the obvious good ones) that have followed. Again, many Christians in today's world have simply gone along for the ride.

Postmodernity has, inevitably, made all this much more confusing. Truth-claims have been unmasked as power-claims. This has then opened the way for all kinds of spin and smear, as the gloves of civilized debate and public discourse come off and all sides try to scratch each other's eyes out with whatever dirty tricks come to hand. Postmodernity has, I believe, the God-given role of announcing to arrogant modernity that all its righteousness was always a mess of filthy rags – in other words, of preaching the secular equivalent of the fall, of total depravity. But it has no gospel, no good news, with which to follow up the bad news. The big stories have been deconstructed into little fragments; the once-powerful notion of the self has been torn apart into competing impulses and prejudices; and truth itself is 'stranger than it used to be'. Notice how well this goes with Gnosticism, and also with empire. It is precisely the gnostic claim that things are not what they seem; that's the insight that made Dan Brown a millionaire several times over. And it is precisely the imperial claim that we, the powerful, create our own truth: truth is what we decide it will be. When Pontius Pilate asked Jesus 'What is truth?', he was expressing his own cynicism at someone else, in a position of utter weakness, having any truth to bear witness to. The only truth, in Pilate's world and increasingly in our own, is what comes out of the barrel of a gun, or the scabbard of a sword.

All this brings us back neatly to chapters 18 and 19 of John's gospel. What might John have to say, through this astonishing conversation of Jesus and Pilate, to the confused and confusing world of our own day?

Jesus, Pilate and the kingdom of God

There are many things that could be said at this point, but I want to focus on the three themes of kingdom, power and truth. The opening exchange between Pilate and the Judaean leaders (18.28–32) looks like a kind of shadow-boxing. Pilate, with his own intelligence networks, surely knew what charge they were proposing to bring; but he wanted to force the Judaean leaders into a concession of their own judicial impotence to deal with what they regarded as a capital charge. Pilate then (18.33–38) asks Jesus directly whether he is 'the King of the Jews': this was the substance of the charge, as we see later in 19.12, where the Judaean leaders declare that 'everyone who makes himself a king is setting himself up against Caesar', which leads directly to their own counter-victory over Pilate. After a preliminary verbal skirmish, Jesus launches in to a description of his 'kingdom', the substance of which is, Yes, I am a king and have a kingdom, but No, it isn't the sort of kingdom you might imagine (18.36).

This is the point at which semi- or crypto-gnostic readings of the text have held sway for a long time, partly due to the King James Version: 'My kingdom is not *of* this world'. This, as we have noted before, is a mistranslation. The Greek speaks of the kingdom being not *ek tou kosmou toutou*, not *from* this world (18.36); that is, the kingdom comes from somewhere else, as Jesus had earlier claimed about himself (8.23), and then, even more strikingly, about his followers as well (17.14). Granted all that we know about Jesus on the one hand and about first-century Jewish kingdom-of-God language on the other (begging, of course, several major questions at this point), we must say that the 'kingdom' of which Jesus was speaking was not *from* this world, but was emphatically *for* this world. It was a kingdom *from* the creator, the one Jesus called 'Father', and consisted of the sovereignty which would replace the usurped sovereignty of 'the ruler of this world' and the human agents which that dark power had employed.

This is, I think, the first and greatest point to be got across in relation not only to contemporary muddles and misunderstandings but to many generations of misreadings of all four canonical gospels. Over against all gnostic attempts, ancient and modern, to turn 'kingdom'-language into a code for other-worldly bliss, this language stubbornly retains its full Jewish sense, world-affirming and indeed world-reclaiming. God's kingdom must come 'on earth as in heaven', and precisely for that reason it is not 'from' this world. That which is only from this world can only imitate the way things are done from within the world. The key example given by Jesus, presupposing that he is a king but demonstrating the difference between his sort of kingdom and all others, is that if his kingdom were from this world *his followers would fight to prevent him being handed over*. This marks almost as radical a departure from normal kingdom-ideas as the gnostic one does, but in a very different direction. In the present world, violence is what kingdoms do. However much they dress it up, sovereignty is enforced; sooner or later that means restraint, and sooner or later restraint means violence. But, as Jesus said to James and John in Mark 10.43, 'It shall not be so among you.'

This point is rammed home with massive though characteristic Johannine irony in the next chapter when Jesus is mocked by the soldiers, crowned with thorns, dressed in purple and hailed as king. The resonances of the next charge – that Jesus made himself to be the son of God (19.7) – are wider, but in the Roman world they amounted to the same thing, since the phrase 'son of God' was in regular use as a key epithet for Caesar. Tiberius was the adopted son of the deified Augustus, as Augustus had been of Julius Caesar. But Caesar's divine rule was implemented by the threat and the use of violence, not by the suffering of it.

Pilate then emphasizes Jesus' kingship, both in his ironic statement and question to the crowd (19.14–15), and then at last, paying them back, in the inscription he places on the cross. Earlier, when Caiaphas had predicted that one man would die for the people, John had commented that this was an unwitting prophecy of Jesus' upcoming redeeming death (11.49–52). John seldom repeats such a hint, and we should be in no doubt what he intends here. When Pilate has the words 'King of the Jews' written out and stuck on Jesus' cross, and when he refuses to alter it, John is emphasizing that Jesus is indeed 'the king of the Jews'. Jesus was the only one who had understood, let alone been obedient to, the strange servant-vocation of the ancient people of God, to whom, as to his own, he had come and had not been received.

And the point about being 'the king of the Jews' is that, in ancient messianic expectation reflecting beliefs and poems about David and Solomon, the ultimate king of the Jews will be the ultimate king of the world. His dominion will be from the one sea to the other, and from the River to the ends of the earth (Psalm 72.8). Early Christianity did not have to shed its Jewish messianism in order to be relevant to the wider world, as so many scholars used to think. It is precisely because they believed Jesus to be the King of the Jews that the early Christians proclaimed him as the world's rightful Lord. In refusing to change the inscription (19.21–22), Pilate has done in his own way what the chief priests had done in theirs; and he had done *to his own status* what they had done to theirs. The chief priests had just said, 'We have no king but Caesar' (19.15), thus stepping down drastically from everything that made Israel Israel (and anticipating the move made by Flavius Josephus a generation later, suggesting that the Roman emperor Vespasian was the fulfilment of scripture's messianic prophecies). Now Pilate declares, however unwittingly, that Jesus is in fact 'the king of the Jews', and is thereby hailing him as the true king, the reality of which Caesar was just a dull and dangerous parody. (Perhaps this is the moment to acknowledge the ancient legend that Pilate was British, in fact Scottish, in fact from St Andrews.)

The account of Jesus' exchange with Pilate is therefore definitely intended by John to emphasize that Jesus, through his crucifixion, was enthroned as the true king of the Jews, the proper lord of the whole world. One might go so far as to say that John and the other three gospels, in their different ways, all intend to tell the story, not of how Jesus died so that we could go to heaven, but of how Jesus died so that he might become the true king of Israel and of the whole world (on this, see *How God Became King* (London: SPCK; San Francisco: HarperOne, 2012)). For John, this is therefore also the moment of Jesus' 'glorification'. This is not at all to overlook the fact that the resurrection, and then the Ascension, are still in the future; not that there is not resurrection, and then Ascension, still to come, but that this is the moment at which, 'having loved his own who were in the world, he loved them to the end' (13.1), the moment when the sovereign, saving love of God which Jesus embodied was on fullest display. John has thus, through his narrative, done what most theologians have failed to do: he has tied tightly together Jesus' embodying and announcing of God's kingdom with Jesus' saving death. Most theologies keep kingdom and cross separate. For John they are part of the same single whole.

Once we have understood what John is saying about the kingdom, with all its breathtaking revolutionary implications, we can ponder the strange words about power in 19.10–11. Pilate, berating Jesus for his silence, asks him, 'Do you not know that I have power to release you, and power to crucify you?' Jesus' answer belongs to the textbook of ancient Jewish monotheism: all earthly power, including that of monstrous pagan tyrants, is ultimately derived from God the creator. 'You would have no power over me unless it had been given you from above.' To have Jesus saying this – Jesus, whom we already recognize as the world's true king! – and saying it to one of Caesar's henchmen, is remarkable indeed; but it resonates not only with much of the rest of ancient Judaism, and also with Paul in Romans 13, but also with, for instance, Polycarp in his dialogue with the tribune who was trying him (see *Martyrdom of Polycarp* 10.2). This is a point that contemporary thought about politics and power has proved unwilling or unable to grasp.

We need to recapitulate the underlying theory at this point. The fact that a particular ruler is wicked, corrupt, monstrous or whatever does not mean, for the ancient Jews and early Christians, that the one creator God has nothing to do with that power. Without making God the author of evil, most ancient Jews and most early Christians believed that God remained sovereign, however much this appeared in the guise of a permissive sovereignty which would then issue (as in the similar point in Isaiah 10) in judgment on those who abused the power thus given to them. But the overall point, as with the kingdom, could hardly be clearer. There is no suggestion, in Jesus' remark, that Pilate is actually quite a good governor, that he is doing his best, that he isn't really to blame (though Jesus does ascribe the 'greater sin' to those who have handed him over (19.11)). The point is that all power belongs to God; or, to put it another way, that order, even tyrannous order, is ultimately better in God's sight than chaos. This is part of a creational theology: God is the God who brings order out of chaos. And this, more specifically, is where Jewish and early Christian political theology derives most obviously from creational and covenantal monotheism: God, having made the world, wants it to be ordered, to prevent wickedness getting out of hand, against the day when he will put everything to rights once and for all. The divinely delegated authority of civil magistrates, even a vacillating, self-serving and cynical one like Pilate, remains at the heart of a biblical doctrine of human authority. (Compare the treatment of human authorities in the book of Acts.)

Once again, however, this context provides part of the meaning which John assigns to the death of Jesus itself. John, like the great storyteller he is, does not rub the point in any further. But his account of Jesus' death has Jesus very much remaining in control: this is his victory, his embodiment and assertion of a power very different from that of Caesar. All Caesar can do is to kill you. God has given Jesus authority to lay down his life and to take it again (10.18); the word for 'authority', *exousia*, is the same in that passage as here. Part of the message of Easter, in the light of the story we have followed to the end of chapter 19, must therefore be that this is the moment when Jesus' *exousia* is unveiled at last. At this point John and Paul are at one: Jesus is 'declared to be Son of God in power through the resurrection of the dead' (Romans 1.4). Now, the reader is to understand, that *exousia* is launched upon the world, so that even though Caesar and his subordinates retain a limited and delegated *exousia*, that of Jesus outshines them and brings them to heel. This is the territory, I suggest, upon which tomorrow's Christians ought to try out fresh and prayerful insights and wisdom as to how public life might be organized, faced as we are with a creaky democracy in which it is often far from clear where any real *exousia* is to be found.

Because of this kingdom, and this power, we can speak at last of truth. In the Farewell Discourses Jesus had spoken of the 'Spirit of Truth' who, coming from the Father, would lead the disciples 'into all the truth' (16.13). The debates about the nature of truth which have surfaced again in postmodernity, after the brittle certainties of modernity (including would-be Christian modernity!), have been exposed as self-serving fictions, but they have nevertheless alerted us thereby to the strangeness of the very concept of truth. Mere correspondence, though important, is obviously not enough – just as mere relationality, which always threatens to collapse into relativism, is even less adequate. Somehow, Jesus seems to be speaking of truth as something which *happens*, which comes into being, under certain circumstances; and the circumstances in question are the obedient living and speaking of genuine human beings, Jesus himself above all.

To understand truth, in fact, you need to hold in mind a version of the entire Christian story. Humans as they stand are bound to reach after truth and to try to use it for their own ends. By this means, they will grasp enough truth to rebuild the Tower of Babel. Postmodernity's protest against arrogant truth-claims thus functions like God coming down to confuse the tongues of the builders. We live with a lot of that confusion right now. But Jesus has come to launch the new creation; the cry 'It is finished' (19.30), we recall, echoes the triumphant completion of Genesis 2.1–2, and John emphasizes in chapter 20 that the resurrection of Jesus takes place on 'the first day of the week'. The problem with 'truth' in the old creation, it seems, is both that creation itself is decaying, will not stay in place, and that the humans who are trying to speak truth about and into that world are distorting it as they do so. What happens in and through Jesus is the redemption of the power of speech, so that Jesus himself can and does witness to the truth, and so that, according to the promise of chapter 16, Jesus' followers will do the same, thereby calling the world and its rulers to account.

This is, in fact, the really challenging thing about John 18 and 19. According to John 16, Jesus' conversation with Pilate will become the template for *the conversation the church must now have with the world*, to implement Jesus' kingdom, to put his *exousia* into effect, to be people who are not only led into all truth but enabled to speak it, especially when it's uncomfortable. The truth is the truth about God's creation, rescued and renewed in Jesus rather than, as in gnostic thought, irrelevant and abandoned. And, as is clear in 18.37, Jesus' claim to be bearing witness to the truth lies at the heart of his claim to be a king. Indeed, it is a central part of his redefinition of what true kingship actually is. To Pilate's question, 'So you are a king?', Jesus' response boils down to this: I have come to tell the truth. That is central to his kingship, and foundational for his new sort of power.

I hope it is thus clear that, at least in compact form, John has given us in these chapters the conceptual tools we need to address in a fresh way the combined challenge our generation is receiving from neo-Gnosticism, neo-imperialism and postmodernity. I would love to think that followers of Jesus in our own day, and indeed any who, while yet agnostic, are prepared to think things through afresh, might try approaching the key issues of today and tomorrow in the light of this biblical vision. I suspect both the recent and the present popes would agree with almost everything I've said, and it might be better to assess their contributions in the light of a framework such as this rather than trying to fit them into the Procrustean bed of journalistic expectations and limitations.

I suspect our politicians past and present would be puzzled by much of what I've said, since it fits neither their messianic idealism nor their shoulder-shrugging pragmatism. In particular, Jesus' definition of his own kingdom in terms of a renunciation of violence should send us back to the events, and the downright lies, of 2003 with sorrow and shame. Millions of Muslims now firmly believe, as many of them did not before, that those who claim the name of Jesus are committed to violence against them. Somehow we have to correct that message. And the supposedly scientific atheism of recent scepticism needs to be confronted with true speech both about the present state of God's creation and about the launching of God's new creation in and through Jesus. That is also the groundplan for a freshly conceived Christian aesthetic, though that is a topic for another time. My claim in this chapter has been that in the remarkable conversation between Jesus and Pilate we can glimpse the outline and contours of a genuinely Christian and biblical view of kingdom, power and truth, and that this glimpse is enough to give us a fresh angle of vision on some of the key problems and challenges that face us in tomorrow's world.

Of course, an angle of vision is not a place to rest content. Vision must turn into speech, and speech into action. 'What is that to you?' said Jesus to Peter when he asked about someone else's vocation. 'You follow me.'

4

God, the earthly powers and terror

The cry 'Where is God?' echoed through the last century. It was heard all the way from the trenches of the First World War to the carpet bombing of the Second, through the Gulag and Auschwitz, through the killing fields of Cambodia and Rwanda and in a million smaller disasters. All these have shown, if any demonstration were needed, that the much-vaunted European Enlightenment of two centuries ago is still a long way from producing liberty, equality and fraternity. Now, with our present century only a few years old, we have already amassed a similar tally, with a similar question. Where was God on September 11, 2001? Where was God in Beslan at the time of the murderous school siege (the question which the broadcaster John Humphries declared had made it impossible for him to believe in God)? Where is God in Lebanon, in the Gaza Strip? Where has God been in Syria and its neighbours, and in the vast number of refugees fleeing for their lives from their homes and countries?

We face these questions at the same time as the UK has faced an unprecedented series of religious issues in its national life. Should Muslim women wear the full *hijab*, or should they conform to Western dress styles? Should Christians, or anybody else, wear crosses in public? Should there be such things as 'faith schools', and if so how should they be regulated? If someone had speculated in the 1980s or 1990s that issues like these would be headline-grabbers in the twenty-first century, we would have laughed. But suddenly all this has come back with a bang on to the public agenda. It is as though the secularists of the 1960s and 1970s, having imagined that religion was in its death throes and that by the end of the century it would have disappeared altogether, are dismayed and angry that this hasn't happened, and are gathering their energies for a new battle against the very idea of religion, against the very rumour of God.

I was talking recently with a leading journalist who suggested one particular analysis of this phenomenon. He reckoned that many now fear that multiculturalism has gone too far, and that it may lead to social and cultural chaos. But because you're not supposed to say this – it wouldn't be 'politically correct' – they are lashing out instead at 'religion', as though it were the real culprit.

People have clearly been doing that on and off for some time, and with good reasons as well as bad ones. After all, a good many of the world's trouble-spots have an inalienable religious dimension, whether it's Northern Ireland or the Balkans, Darfur or the North-West Frontier, not to mention the Middle East. This argument now regularly goes round in circles, since some of last century's greatest atrocities, notably the Gulag and the Holocaust, stood in the ignoble tradition of the French Revolution itself, killing for reasons of militant atheism. In other words, yes, religions can become dangerous ideologies; but so can irreligions. Our politicians and media have resolutely refused to acknowledge that there is a religious dimension to all human life, let alone that it's possible to study how this works, to distinguish healthy religion from harmful religion, and to work for a creative synthesis of faith and public life. There is a world of difference between an open and generous secular world where people of every point of view are free to find fresh ways of living and working together, and a secular*ist* world which does its best to banish the rumour of God from the public square altogether. This is a lesson, incidentally, that any university worth the name has to learn again and again – though at the moment it seems that many university campuses are doing their best to ban speakers who say things some people might find offensive. We urgently need to address this in our wider public life, and universities and similar settings are good places to get into practice.

Anyway, all of these remarkable and in some ways unprecedented questions set a context which makes it simultaneously more urgent and more difficult to unravel the various threads which go to make up the problem of where God might be found in relation to the so-called 'War on Terror'. Let me now try to lay out some of these threads and suggest how they are getting tangled up, before moving to some positive proposals in the second and third parts of this chapter. There are dozens of strands to this; I here briefly highlight only five.

To begin with, there is the problem of understanding where we are in the Western world and culture as a whole. The convenient broad-brush labels of 'modernity' and 'postmodernity', which refer to two different moods and controlling narratives rather than two chronologically dateable periods of cultural history, point towards one kind of mapping exercise in politics as well as culture. The self-perception of the Western world two hundred years ago was that we were the enlightened ones. Our science, technology, philosophy and democracy had moved us to a point where we had not just the possibility but the obligation to spread our freedom, justice and peace as far as our imperial ambitions could take us, extracting of course the usual financial price, backed up with the usual military force.

As a Roman historian, I have a sense of *déjà vu* at this point: this is precisely how the Romans argued as they spread their empire from Britain to the Black Sea and beyond. All empires claim that they possess justice, freedom and peace and that they have a duty to share these things with everybody else. And part of our current problem is that though the postmodern turn in philosophy and culture has sneered at this great imperial dream, it hasn't been able to shake it. Indeed, empires characteristically use the weapons of deconstruction to ward off challenges, as Downing Street allowed documents to be massaged and spun this way and that in its efforts to persuade us that the War on Terror, and the war on Iraq, were morally justified. Thus both with modernity and with postmodernity we have lost our moral bearings in our dealings with the world, and it's not surprising that we find ourselves flailing around and unsure why things are still going wrong, let alone what to do about them. In particular, current terrorism is a deeply postmodern phenomenon, but we're using the thoroughly modernist weapons of normal military might to counter it. No wonder we're not getting very far.

Furthermore, as I argued in the first chapter of *Evil and the Justice of God* (London: SPCK; Downers Grove, IL: InterVarsity Press, 2004), the leaders of the Western world have adopted an incredibly naive and shallow analysis of the problem of evil itself. They act as if they'd assumed that the world's problems were basically solved, that all we needed was a bit more free trade and parliamentary-style democracy, and then any remaining pockets of evil would wither away. So the reaction to the attacks of September 11, 2001 was astonishingly immature: 'Goodness, there seems to be some serious evil out there after all! What on earth shall we do? I know – let's go and drop some bombs on it; that'll sort it out!' Well, the American people finally said in 2006 (in the senatorial elections which showed a strong reaction against George W. Bush) what lots of us were saying back in 2002: that was not and is not the way to deal with things. Evil is more radical and powerful than that. What's more, the line between good and evil doesn't lie between 'us' and 'them', but runs as a jagged line through each human being and each human society. We – and I include the churches on both sides of the Atlantic – have often colluded with a spurious and inadequate analysis of what's wrong in the world and what can be done about it. That's the first strand in our problem.

The second strand is closely related. In our idolization of modern secular democracy we have imagined that, provided our leaders attain power by a popular vote, that's all that matters, and that the only possible critique is to vote them out again next time round. But that wasn't how the early Christians and their Jewish contemporaries saw things. They weren't particularly concerned with how people in power came to be in power. They were extremely concerned with how those in power exercised that power; and, to that end, they believed in speaking the truth to power, in calling the principalities and powers to account, reminding them that they hold power as a trust from the God who made the world and before whom they must stand to explain themselves.

The urgent political question we face has to do with global structures of governance and policing. The United Nations is a creaky organization, partly because some of its members worry about its becoming strong enough to hold them to account. Yet the War on Terror, and the engagements in Iraq and Afghanistan, have demonstrated beyond reasonable doubt that the USA (with a little help from the UK) does not and cannot constitute a credible global police force. Why, for a start, aren't we tackling dangerous and abusive leaders in North Korea, or Zimbabwe, as well? As long as we can be portrayed as the 'Christian' West attacking the 'Muslim' Middle East, everything we do is bound to be counter-productive. Not to realize this – and the architects of the War on Terror have studiously ignored it – is culpable self-willed ignorance. This second strand, then, is a confusion about what healthy democracy itself might look like.

Third, there is the rise of contemporary Islam. Islam has been an enormous force for civilization in the world – including the preservation of some of the world's greatest philosophical and cultural texts. We shouldn't forget that for many centuries in many countries

Muslims have lived alongside Jews and Christians in peace, social harmony, and even mutual respect and affection. The great majority of Muslims in the UK today want that to be the case, not least because they believe that their religion commits them to it. Sadly, a minority around the world, for more complex reasons than most Western commentators allow, has reacted furiously to events in the Middle East, as much to the alliance of the Saudi rulers with the USA as to the situation in Israel and Palestine. As the terrorist activities of a very small number have grown in importance, the Western powers have played into their hands by reacting in immature and counter-productive ways. Every bomb dropped has proved to be another recruiting agent for Al Qaeda or Isil. Meanwhile, the efforts of many to build bridges between communities, and to rediscover what it is that mainstream Muslims believe and why, has been far too little and far too late. To react to sudden drastic events by declaring Islam to be a wicked and violent religion, as some have done, simply makes matters worse. This is not to say, of course, that Islam and Christianity are basically the same. They are not. But to sketch out or even highlight those differences is not to say that we must come to blows. Rather, it is to say that we must find ways to live together in the same communities despite those differences.

Fourth, there is the problem of violence itself, and of war itself. Western culture has oscillated between the high moral tone of pacifism and the self-righteous anger which decides that *these* enemies are so wicked that they must be bombed. We sometimes appeal to the old 'just war' theory, but usually to support decisions reached on other grounds, often nakedly pragmatic. I don't hear, in our public discourse, much evidence that our leaders have reflected at any depth on whether, and if so when, some force is necessary, and how that force should be organized, applied and regulated. The question of the legality of bombing Iraq in 2003 was notorious at the time and over a decade later the issue is still in doubt. Until that kind of discussion at least begins, then all questions of war, let alone a war against *terror*, merely bounce to and fro around the hollow space where there should be a reasoning public mind and where, instead, we have the stale alternatives of political correctness and political expediency.

As a subset of this fourth problem, I draw attention to the fact that the very notion of a 'War on Terror' strikes a false note. It wasn't actually invented by George W. Bush and his colleagues. Bill Clinton and other earlier presidents used similar language, and the Western powers engaged in military action against terrorists and those who harbour them long before September 11, 2001. But the oddity of the notion itself, and the illogicality of actions which were bound to encourage terrorism rather than quieten it down, should tell us we're in a moral mess. Rather than think things out properly, we have relied on the same methods as we used in the nineteenth century: if in doubt, send in the gunboats and teach Johnny Foreigner a lesson he won't forget. In fact, the only real way to fight terror is by working for mutual understanding and respect – winning hearts and minds, which is often said but not often done. Throwing stones at a wasp's nest because one wasp has come out and stung you is not the best way of addressing, let alone solving, the problem. President Obama's 2013 statement that 'we must define our effort not as a boundless "Global War on Terror", but rather as a series of persistent, targeted efforts to dismantle specific networks of violent extremists that threaten America' may represent a level of improvement in understanding, but this change of language hasn't made a lot of difference on the ground.

In particular, alas, many in the West still seem to suppose that violence can be redemptive. The 'Superman' myth, or the 'Captain America' complex, has been shown to underlie the implicit narratives of generation after generation of American leaders, generating the belief that the hero must use redemptive violence to restore the town, the country, the world to its proper state. (See Robert Jewett and John Shelton Lawrence, *Captain America and the Crusade Against Evil: The Dilemma of Zealous Nationalism*, and, by the same authors, *The Myth of the American Superhero* (both Grand Rapids: Eerdmans, 2002).) Unless we address this, peace will remain a romantic dream, while the world – the world in which the next generations will hope to bring up their families – becomes increasingly dangerous.

The fifth and most important problem is that we have all forgotten how to talk about God in public. Increasingly, over the last two centuries, such talk has been regarded as a category mistake. God and public life have been kept separate, both by devout Christians who supposed that mixing faith and politics would corrupt faith, and by devout secularists who supposed that mixing them would corrupt politics. You can't keep up this kind of dualism for long, especially in times of crisis. But, unless you think it through, the two will rush back together in unhealthy combinations. During the Cold War, many Americans believed that God had raised up their country to be a bastion against atheistic communism. Behind the 'War on Terror' is the lineal descendant of that warped and dangerous idea, with Islam taking the place of communism – an idea embraced all the more eagerly because some Islamic nations just happen to possess oil, and some Islamic extremists just happen to fly planes into buildings. This in turn has given extra impetus to the belief, powerful in the USA (but not many other places) for quite different reasons, that the present State of Israel is the fulfilment of Old Testament prophecy, so that Israel must be supported right or wrong. This doctrine is as dangerous in terms of politics as it is unwarranted in terms of biblical exegesis.

It is ironic that, in the UK, those who have brought God back into politics have tended to be on the left of the spectrum, while those who've done it in the USA have tended to be in the new Christian right. In the UK, grumpy letters telling clergy not to meddle in politics come from retired colonels in Tunbridge Wells; in the USA, similar messages come from semi-Marxist anti-globalization protesters. All too often we simply see a Christian overlay on top of social, cultural and political agendas generated from elsewhere. It's not easy to avoid this trap entirely, but we are all called to try. (On all this, see James Davidson Hunter, *To Change the World: The Irony, Tragedy and Possibility of Christianity in the Late Modern World* (Oxford: OUP, 2010).)

So where is God in the middle of all this? Opinion on that question has largely been divided between two viewpoints, more or less equally misguided.

On the one hand, some have insisted that God has little or nothing to do with politics, since God is much more interested in saving souls for a disembodied eternity than with political problems on this earth. People often remind me that Jesus said his kingdom was 'not of this world'. Actually, as we saw in the previous chapter, what Jesus said was that his kingdom was not *from* this world. The kingship which Jesus brings does not originate with the world the way it presently is, but is certainly intended by God *for* this world – otherwise why do we pray, in the Lord's Prayer, that God's kingdom will come 'on earth as in heaven'? The type of conservative Christianity represented by the 'not of this world' viewpoint has, in my view and in Paul's words, a zeal for God which is not according to knowledge, being ignorant of God's justice and seeking merely to establish its own (Romans 10.3). In this view, God and the world are to be held at arm's length. True Christianity then consists in escaping from the present world into a personal and private spirituality for the moment and an other-worldly salvation for an eternal future.

On the other hand, many go to war, including the 'War on Terror', insisting that God is on their side. This is said less frequently in the USA than it was a few years ago, and it hasn't of course been said by political leaders in the UK. But it has been a common strand in many wars and many places. Against this we cite another well-known biblical text, that human wrath does not bring about God's justice (James 1.20).

Where then is God in our world, in our wars, in our weeping?

Speaking of God, speaking of the world

The question, How to speak of God in the same breath as the War on Terror, is clearly a subset of the question, How to speak of God at all, and, more particularly, How to speak of God in relation to the world as a whole.

Many otherwise intelligent and well-read people in our culture assume that there are only two possible answers to these questions. (There are, obviously, other options. Atheism denies that there is a question to be addressed; agnosticism denies that we can say anything much about it; pantheism proposes that God and the world are more or less the same thing.) Most people in our culture still assume that the word 'God' is more or less univocal, referring to a being located at some distance from our space-time universe, and that the options are *either* that this God keeps his distance and doesn't 'intervene' within the world *or* that this God does sometimes reach in to the world from the outside and do things which can be called 'intervention'.

Many Christians believe themselves committed to the second view. Without it, they might think they had an absent God, and they wouldn't be able to explain things like the resurrection – not to mention their strong sense that God has 'intervened' in their own lives, with rescue, healing, transformation and challenge. But many people today, including many Christians, are deeply uncomfortable with this model of 'intervention'. If God 'intervenes' to cure someone's cancer, or to raise Jesus from the dead, why didn't he 'intervene' to stop the Holocaust, or the road accident? People sometimes speak and write as if God had intervened personally to stop Hitler winning the Second World War, but I would find it difficult to explain that to a Syrian refugee whose home had been destroyed and whose family were clinging to a lifeboat somewhere in the Mediterranean Sea.

This puzzle of how to speak about God's relation to the world, and these regular alternative answers – either God never intervenes in the world, looking on impotently while we make a mess of things, or he sometimes does, in which case we want to know why he doesn't do it more often – plays out in the debate about God and the War on Terror. Either God is keeping his distance, so that attempts to invoke him either on the side of Islamist terror or American counter-terror are simply a category mistake. Or God does sometimes intervene, and the question is then more complicated: is he on one side rather than the other? Is he with the terrorists, or with the victims of terror? Is he with the aggressors, or the thousands of innocent victims of Western aggression? Or should he be 'intervening' in some other way, to rebuke both sides and stop the madness, and if so how?

At its best, the Christian tradition has rejected this either–or model and has proposed something significantly different. From the very beginning Christians have said that while we don't know all that much about God's own inner being, we discover who God is, and what he is up to in the world, as we look at Jesus of Nazareth. Of course, that can seem to compound the problem. If you put Jesus into the falsely polarized either–or I just spoke of, you will end up saying either that Jesus was just a good man, or that he was a kind of invader from outer space. But the early Christian writings suggest a different approach. They insisted that Jesus was just as fully a human being as he was fully divine. Everything about him (his words, his deeds, his self-awareness so far as we can probe it historically) indicates that he saw himself not as an isolated individual out of the blue, but as the one who completed and fulfilled a long and winding story, of how the creator God had decided to heal his wounded creation, to rescue his rebel subjects, not by simply acting upon it and them from the outside, nor by hoping the world would sort itself out without his help, but by acting *from within the world* to put the world to rights at the last. The story of Israel, set out graphically and often tragically in the Old Testament, presents itself as this kind of story. Pondering it, we begin to see why.

If it is true that there is a good God who was responsible for making the world in the first place, it would be a denial of his own character if, in order to rescue the world from its threatened lapse into chaos, he acted upon it in such a way as to deny the goodness, the order and the structure, of the world itself. Rather, relying on one of the good features of the original creation itself, the fact that human beings were made in God's own image, called to reflect him within the world, God called a family of human beings through whom, even though they themselves were part of the problem, he would eventually act in such a way as to restore and heal his world. It was this family, the children of Abraham, Isaac and Jacob, whose story Jesus of Nazareth believed himself to be bringing to completion. This is the story we need if we are to understand what the Christian claims about Jesus really mean, not least in relation to the troubles of the world.

At the same time, Jesus seems to have believed (and his earliest followers explored this enthusiastically) that because the story of Israel, and its coming to its God-ordained climax, was the divinely intended way of putting the world to rights, this plan turned out to be a plan designed for God's own use. It is as though a composer were to write a violin concerto knowing that he and he alone would be able to play the solo part, and that it would exactly express his own deepest musical wisdom. It is this double sense, of Jesus as the climax of the story of Israel and *therefore also* as the climax of the story of God, that goes to the heart of what Jesus himself believed and what his first followers struggled to put into words. This is how we can say, without lapsing into the language either of intervention-from-outside or of non-intervention-from-outside, that Jesus was both fully human and fully divine.

But Jesus didn't come as it were merely to display what God looked like in human form. The problem of the world, and of humans, cannot be reduced to lack of information. Jesus came with a job to do, to complete the work to which Israel was called. This work, from the call of Abraham onwards, was to put the human race to rights, and so to put the whole creation to rights. (This is a controversial way to read scripture, but I have argued for it in detail elsewhere.) As St Paul put it: God was in the Messiah, reconciling the world to himself (2

Corinthians 5.19). As the gospel writers tell the story, this task was to be accomplished, not simply by revealing to the world who God really was, still less by offering an example of how human beings really ought to live. It was to be accomplished by Jesus bringing about, within this present world, the sovereign, healing rule of the creator God. Jesus was addressing the question, 'What might it look like if God was running this show?' and answering, 'This is what it looks like: just watch.' And then, 'just listen'. In what he did, and in the stories he told to explain what he was doing, Jesus was announcing and inaugurating what he and his contemporaries referred to as 'the kingdom of God', the long-awaited hope that the creator God would run the whole show, on earth as in heaven.

But the problem was, and still is, that other people were and still are running the show. Other kingdoms, other power structures, have usurped the rule of the world's wise creator, and the forces of evil they have unleashed are exceedingly powerful and destructive. Jesus' task of inaugurating God's kingdom therefore necessarily led him to meet those other forces in direct combat, to draw upon himself their full, dark fury in order to exhaust their power and make a way through, so that despite their force the creator's project of new creation would at last be launched. That is one clue at least to the meaning of Jesus' crucifixion, as many New Testament writers indicate; though that event, planting the sign of God's kingdom in the middle of space, time and matter, remains inexhaustible. But let's be clear. As the gospels tell the story, Jesus' death was the culmination of several different strands: a political process, a religious clash, a spiritual war, all rushing together into one terrible day, one terrible death. And in the light of that, according to Jesus himself and his first followers, everything in the world looks different, *is* different, and must be approached differently. With Jesus' death, the power structures of the world were called to account. With his resurrection, a new life, a new power, was unleashed upon the world. And the question is, how ought this to work out? What should we be doing as a result?

I hope it is clear how the presence of Jesus in the middle of the question of 'God and the world' gives that question a quite different shape. It isn't a question of *either* God keeping his distance from a world in which he is absent *or* deciding from time to time to 'intervene' from the outside. It is, rather, a matter of God being *both* utterly outside and beyond the world – God is a different kind of existence altogether – *and* personally present and active within it. And that activity is not, as it were, a matter of Jesus striding around doing impossible things to prove how divine he was. Rather, Jesus' powerful actions are all about the breaking in of new creation into the world of the old – a new creation in which the creator's original intention is fulfilled, through signs which point forward to the day when God will eventually make all things new, put all things to rights, and wipe away all tears from all eyes. The challenge is to place the fact of Jesus into the middle of our picture of God and the world, and to ask the key questions, the hard questions, afresh in that light.

As we do that, we discover one thing in particular. The God who comes to the middle of world history in Jesus does not come to wave a magic wand and automatically cure everything in sight. The God who comes to the middle of history comes to take its pain and shame, its guilt and rebellion, on to himself, to bear the weight of the world's evil so that the world may be healed. This is not an incidental detail in the picture. It is what gives significance and shape to the whole. It means that whenever we ask the question of where God is in the world – whether in the world in general, or in the Tsunami or the Holocaust or the War on Terror – we should look first for God where the night is darkest and the pain is worst, not in the blaze of glory and the blast of trumpets but in the cry of the baby and the scream of the tortured. And that will colour our reflections from this point on.

But before we can turn to the third and final section of this chapter, let me reflect on the earliest Christian sense of *vocation*. Jesus' first followers believed that they were called to put into effect what he had achieved in principle; that, if you like, they were to go out and act the play he had written, to sing the song he had composed. He had achieved the victory of the creator God over the forces that were destroying and distorting creation; he had launched God's project of new creation. Now they had to go into a world still dominated by the anti-creation powers, and in the power of Jesus' Spirit to make new creation happen. All Christian thinking about God and the world, therefore, must include not only Jesus himself, bearing the world's pain and launching the world's renewal, but also the promise of God's Spirit, active in the world both through Jesus' followers and out beyond them. The God-and-world question, in other words, needs to be rephrased in terms of the Trinity. Indeed, to realize this is to realize that the Trinity, so far from being a dry and dusty dogma that nobody understands, is at the heart of the fresh understanding of God and the world we badly need today.

With all this in mind, then, I turn back to the question of God and the War on Terror. What happens when we rethink the question in the light of a Trinitarian understanding of God and the world?

God, the powers and the war

To begin with, let me map out as simply as possible what Christianity and indeed Judaism has regularly (not always, but usually) thought and taught about political power. There are four moves to be made, in this rough sketch of a Christian political theology.

First, the creator God wants the world to be ordered, not chaotic. The order in question is to be a human order: that is to say, God intends that there should be human structures of government. God does not want anarchy. Just as God intends the world of plants and crops to work under human management, so God intends that human societies should be wisely ordered under human stewardship. This pattern, of delegated authority if you like, goes all the way back to the human vocation to be God's 'image-bearers'. It corresponds to the pattern of God's action in and through Jesus Christ. That is what Paul says in Colossians 1.15–17.

The alternative to the rule of human beings is that you have either anarchy or unmediated theocracy. This unpleasant dichotomy has given us our present fixation on what we think of as left-wing and right-wing political leanings. If we could only understand how these have grown up within that false theological antithesis I spoke of earlier, we might be able ourselves to grow up beyond the sterile to-and-fro of our present Western political life. But that's another story.

But, second, if God intends that there should be power structures; if he wills that humans should find ways of running their world and bringing it to wise order – then, within a world in rebellion, this call to power translates all too easily into a temptation to the abuse of power. As soon as you make someone a steward of creation (a member of parliament, a monarch, a town councillor, the chair of a charity, or even a bishop!), you challenge them to navigate past the temptation to use that power for their own advantage, to become, in other words, part of the problem to which they are supposed to be part of the solution. God wants his rebel world to be ordered, to be under authorities and governments, because otherwise the bullies and the arrogant will always prey on the weak and the helpless; but all authorities and governments face the temptation to become bullies and arrogant themselves. The New Testament writers, like other Jews at the time, saw this magnified in the Roman empire of their day. Those with eyes to see can see it magnified, if anything even larger, in other subsequent empires right down to our own day.

Third, therefore, it is part of the inalienable task of God's people, of those who worship the creator God, whom we see in Jesus and know through the Spirit, to speak the truth to power. This calling will mean reminding governments, local councillors, authorities in every sphere, including church leaders, of *their* calling to selfless stewardship. It will mean pointing out fearlessly (but also humbly: arrogance will spoil the whole thing) where this trust is being abused, in whatever way. Once more, God is not nearly so interested in how rulers get to be rulers as he is in how they behave as rulers. That is why the church has the vital task of reminding them of their proper vocation and of calling them to account. (One of the problems in the Western world today is that, by and large, the media and the journalists think this is *their* task, and so try to elbow the church out of the territory they have taken over. But they are themselves just as much in need of critique as anyone else.)

But, fourth and in particular, it is the task of the followers of Jesus to remind those called to authority, in whatever sphere, that the God who made the world intends to put the world to rights at the last. It isn't simply a matter of reminding the authorities of duties they have always had. It is a matter of calling them to acts of justice and mercy which will anticipate, in the present time, God's final setting of all things to rights, God's wiping away of every tear from every eye. This calling – which many authorities and rulers dimly recognize, though many alas glimpse it and turn away to more seductive options – is, whether people recognize it or not, the call to live under the lordship of Jesus Christ. In his death and resurrection, Jesus has claimed that sovereignty over them; and the followers of Jesus must therefore issue the call to implement the victory he won over evil, over hatred, over violence and death itself, and thereby to *anticipate* in the present time, always partially and fitfully but none the less truly, the eventual victory of God's loving, restorative justice.

The doing of justice and mercy in the present time by those called to power locally, nationally and globally is thus to be seen within the framework of the historical victory of Jesus in his death and resurrection and of the future, coming, final victory of God over all evil, all violence, all arrogant abuse of power. Where the world's rulers and authorities genuinely strive for that end – to implement the victory of Jesus, to anticipate the final victory of God – the Christian church declares, as the ancient Jews did with the pagan king Cyrus, that God's Spirit is at work, whether the rulers know it or not. And naturally, for that reason, the way in which Jesus' followers articulate this call will vary according to the receptivity or otherwise of the rulers. It's no good saying 'Jesus is telling you to do this' to someone who has no time for Jesus. But if the church can translate what we believe Jesus would say into the language, and the coherent arguments, of the wider world then such obedience can become a possibility.

We have thus arrived at a preliminary answer to the question, Where is God in the power politics of the world? God is present, calling rulers and authorities to account, and acting through them to anticipate the day when his justice and mercy will be seen in all the earth, when the earth shall be filled with his glory as the waters cover the sea. Within this framework, what can and should we say about God and the War on Terror?

This at least should be clear: that we are not saying either that God is absent, at best looking on from a great distance, or that God is present, simply fighting on one side or the other. If we are to think Christianly – and I recognize that for many readers that may be an open question, but it is important at least see how a Christian might be supposed to think – then we must think according to the pattern of Jesus Christ. And that means that the first place we should look for God in the War on Terror would be in the smouldering ruins of the Twin Towers, in the tears of the widows and children on that terrible day, and then in the ruins of Baghdad and Basra, the shattered homes and lives of the tens of thousands who have, through no fault of their own, been in the wrong place at the wrong time as the angry superpower, like a rogue elephant teased by a little dog, has gone on the rampage, stamping on everything that moves in the hope of killing the dog by killing everything within reach, to be followed in turn by the wild ravages of Isil in Homs and Kirkuk.

The presence of God within the world at a time of war must be calibrated according to what Paul says in Romans 8, that the Spirit groans within God's people as they groan with the pain of the world. The cross of Jesus Christ is the sign and the assurance that the God who made the world still loves the world and, in that love, groans and grieves:

> And when human hearts are breaking
> under sorrow's iron rod,
> then they find that self-same aching
> deep within the heart of God.
> (From the hymn 'God is love,
> let heaven adore him' by
> Timothy Rees (1874–1939))

If my analysis is anything like correct, we should also see God in the calling to account of those who abuse power, in the reminding of the rulers and authorities that they have a task of justice and mercy, anticipating God's eventual rule and implementing the achievement of Jesus.

But, in particular, we must face the deeply ambiguous question of the present power and position of the USA. I have said it before and will say it again: I am not anti-American when I criticize some policies of some American leaders, any more than I am anti-British when I criticize some of the policies of my own elected leaders. To suggest otherwise is simply a cheap way of avoiding the real questions. I believe that the creator God allows human societies to rise and fall, human empires to grow and wane, and that, though of course things are massively more complicated than this, we could see in the rise of the USA as the current sole superpower some great possibilities for bringing justice and mercy, genuine freedom and prosperity, to the whole world. Empires always carry that possibility. But, alas, empires also, for the same reason, face the temptation to use their power for their own prestige and wealth. It doesn't take a PhD in macroeconomics or political theory to see that this has been massively the case in the rise of the present global empire – an empire in which, undeniably, we British share to quite an extent. The challenge now, and one of the central answers to the question 'Where is God in the War on Terror?', is this: to provide (a) a critique of American empire without implying that the world should collapse into anarchy, and

(b) a fresh sense of direction for that empire without colluding with massive abuses of power.

First, we must work from every angle either to enable the United Nations and the International Courts of Justice to function as they should, or to replace them with something else that can do the same job better. The only way we could have done something wise in Iraq would have been with a force with the energy of the whole international community behind it, composed equally of Norwegians and Nigerians, of Australians and Pakistanis, of Chileans and Japanese, of Saudis, Lebanese, Indians . . . and, yes, British and Americans. To continue to resist the making real of such an internationally credible police force, as many on the right in the USA have done, is more and more obviously a way of saying that now that we're in power we will use that power utterly for our own advantage, and rule out the possibility that anyone might call us in turn to account. Of course, when China or India becomes the next superpower, we can expect the present superpower to go running for help to any international court that might then exist.

But the point is this: it is time to make the transition globally that we in Britain made in the 1830s when we moved from local militias to a credible national police force. Clearly, with any such move there are all the same dangers of the abuse of power. But we already have abuse of power. It is part of the church's task, in calling present abuse to account, to work for a better structure which could credibly deal with all kinds of problems around the world. I wish I thought that such a refreshed United Nations was likely to emerge soon. The vested interests against such a thing are powerful indeed. But we must work and pray for something like this to happen. In such work, and in such prayer, God is present to call both the War on Terror, and the Terror itself, to account.

But, second, there is a task which involves us all, at every level. Terrorism arises principally and obviously because individuals and groups sense themselves to be alienated from ordinary process, unable by any imaginable means to effect changes for which they long, locally or globally. The roots of present terrorist movements have been much studied, and they are more complex than politicians and the media often imply. But the way to make sure that the causes of terror are diminished and if possible eliminated altogether is not – of course it is not! – to drop bombs on potential terrorists until they get the point. That is to fight one kind of terror with another, which not only keeps terror in circulation but stirs up yet more. The way to eliminate the causes of terror is to seize every opportunity to work together, to talk together, to discover what makes people tick within worldviews quite unlike our own, and in short – as was said by the armies in Iraq, but without much visible effect – to win hearts and minds, not necessarily to a Christian worldview, certainly not to a modern secular Western worldview, but to a shared worldview of common humanity, incorporating what the great majority of human beings want, genuine justice and genuine peace. Part of the task of the church in this generation is, I believe, to encourage all those who are working in this way, and to remind our politicians and our media that this is the direction we all ought to be travelling.

Where then is God in the War on Terror? Grieving and groaning within the pain and horror of his battered but still beautiful world. Stirring in the hearts of human beings the desire for a more credible structure of global justice and mercy. Burning into the imagination of human beings a hope that peace and reconciliation might eventually triumph over suspicion and hatred, that the world may be put to rights and that we may anticipate that in the present time. The present generation, especially its younger members, faces a new world, full of possibilities for great good and great ill. I have argued here that the Christian gospel, revealing the mysterious God we discover in Jesus and the Spirit, offers a robust and rigorous framework for discerning where God is at work in the midst of the dangers and opportunities that confront us. All of us in our different callings are summoned to this task; some, perhaps, to make it their life's work. Jesus is Lord. The Spirit is powerful. God is doing a new thing. Let's get out there and join in.

5

Power, faith and the law

Signs of the times

I begin with two signs of our times. The media are always on the lookout for statements by leading members of the clergy that they can take out of context and then complain about, and in 2008 some newspapers had a field day with a lecture by Rowan Williams, then Archbishop of Canterbury. In his carefully argued piece, he pointed out that in our plural society the British law had already been adjusted to make it possible, in carefully defined contexts, for some elements of Islamic financial law to be taken into account. He was then accused, absurdly, of wanting to introduce sharia law into the UK. All sorts of issues arise from this incident, and I here focus on three.

First, quite simply, the Archbishop didn't say what the media said he said. His real offence was that he had presumed to challenge the media's vice-like control on public opinion, and so was being called arrogant and patronizing by people who don't want reasoned discourse and prefer only catchy soundbites. The media, which supposedly make it possible for people across the country to hear what leaders are saying, sometimes in fact make it impossible.

The second issue raised by Archbishop Rowan's speech was his careful deconstruction of the Enlightenment myth of secular progress and its accompanying political discourse. In this respect, he stands in line, more or less, with Professor John Gray (*Straw Dogs*, *False Dawn*, *Heresies*, etc.). He pointed out on the one hand the religious and indeed Christian roots of the Enlightenment's vision of justice and rights, and on the other the way in which the secularist rhetoric, growing ever more shrill these days, effectively cuts off the branch of Reason on which it claims to be sitting – as, again, we see in the media reaction. And with this deconstruction he was challenging the monopolistic idea of a secular state, and he was doing so in the name, not of an arrogant faith elbowing its way into the public domain, but as part of the inner logic of the Christian-derived Enlightenment vision itself. The danger he had in mind was that of a state which could pass laws of increasing severity to constrict not only what religious people may do but what they may say and how they may think. The slogan *vox populi vox Dei* ('The voice of the people is the voice of God') may have begun as a cry for liberty from clerical oppression, but it quickly turns into a new form of self-justifying tyranny, seeking (as we shall see presently) to prevent religious belief from having any effect on public life.

One of the ironies here, clearly, is that the very secularists who are insisting that there must be one identical law for everyone about everything do not want to live by that when it comes to, say, the blasphemy laws, the fact of the Established Churches in England and Scotland, or the present ban on euthanasia. We are living in a clash of ideologies, as secular liberalism seeks a uniform (and uniformly non-religious) public life, and secular communitarianism insists on every 'identity' being validated (except, often enough, religious identities).

This points to the third issue raised by Archbishop Rowan: the place of Islam and its legal codes within a contemporary plural society. He was arguing against a state-sponsored and state-regulated form of multiculturalism in which only those aspects of cultures which fit in to current secular thinking are permitted, and for a recognition of 'multiple affiliations' within what he called an 'interactive pluralism'. He was not recommending parallel jurisdictions, as some in the media imagined. He was simply suggesting that some aspects of traditional Islamic law might find their way into the realm of permitted local options, as indeed had already begun to happen.

The questions that then arise are well known within the family of churches to which I belong, the Anglican Communion. How do you know which local options are to be allowed? On what grounds? and Who says? To get underneath questions like that in his broader discussion, the Archbishop raised the notions of 'human dignity as such' and of 'shared goods and priorities'. One might have thought these would be welcome in all contexts, but what he said was disturbing because he insisted on locating them within a universe of discourse larger than that of secularism. Secularism invokes the grandiose vision of the Enlightenment. But, as the Archbishop's deconstructive argument showed, it loses its apparent moral force by claiming too much (that it will solve all the problems of cultural plurality) and by denying the very ground on which it stands (that of the Western Christian tradition). Interestingly, Pope Benedict XVI said something similar in his speech to the United Nations in New York on 18 April in that same year, 2008.

The Archbishop's lecture clearly touched several raw nerves in our culture. When that happens at the dentist, we know it's going to be painful but we also know we need to get things sorted out. The reaction, as much as the speech itself, tells us that all is not well in our confused culture.

The second sign of the times to which I draw attention is the decline of democracy. In a 2007 article in the *Times Literary Supplement*, Professor Vernon Bogdanor sketched the ways in which contemporary Western democracy is under threat, not so much from absolutist terrorism, which threatens life and limb but not systems of government, but from within. Democracy is the current Western answer to the problem of how to avoid chaos without lapsing into tyranny, and vice versa. But we cannot assume that just because people are able to vote every once in a while that means that we have the balance right. In fact, there are several signs of chaos on the one hand (such as the unfettered rule of multinational companies and banks), and of tyranny on the other (such as the imposition of new and fierce regulations designed to stop people living out their faith). One such example would be the refusal of the Appeal Court to uphold the right of a Sheffield magistrate to abstain from handling cases of same-sex couples adopting children. Even though the laws in these areas are quite new, and would have been unthinkable less than a generation ago, some of the newspapers that commented on that story insisted loudly that the same law must now apply to all. No exceptions were to be allowed. To many, this looks like a new type of tyranny. And if one wants further examples of chaos, one need look no further than the European Union, where, behind the glossy façade, there are decades-long unresolved financial problems and, in very recent times, multiple confusions on what to do about the influx of refugees, on how to cope with global terrorism, and so on.

All this calls into question the normal Western assumption that if only we could spread our style of democracy around the rest of the world it would solve problems in all directions. One could draw the same conclusion from the way in which Western democracies currently operate. One need only look at the enormous time, attention and money devoted to an entire year's worth of electioneering in the USA, not to mention the fact that, though an incoming president of the USA will have effective power over the whole world, it's only Americans who get to vote. Part of the problem in the Middle East – at least, part of the present shape of the problem, since the problems themselves go back many centuries – is that when the so-called 'Arab Spring' was launched in 2010/11 most Western leaders and journalists believed that it would simply be a matter of deposing tyrants and allowing freedom and democracy to emerge, as though democracy were the natural state of affairs, with tyranny being an artificial brake on it. In fact, as we now know, this approach means that we have merely colluded with the swapping of tyranny for chaos. Things are more complicated than we had imagined. As Archbishop Rowan said about law, human dignity and shared goods and priorities, so it is with democracy. They don't just happen.

The former Secretary General of the UN, Kofi Annan, insisted in his retirement speech that democracies, like all other rulers, need to be called to account, both in what they actually do and in what they actually are. Simply voting every few years – though that is a whole lot better than not voting every few years! – is not a very effective way of achieving this. In the UK, the majority of parliamentary seats are 'safe', so that the real 'election' takes place behind closed doors in a small room where the local party activists choose their candidate. We will only recover a sense of genuine participation, and hence the reality of democracy, when we deconstruct some of the grandiose claims that have been made or implied, and rethink our social and political practices from the root up. And part of that root, in the Western world at least, comes from the Judaeo-Christian tradition, in ways which I shall explore presently. (To anticipate objections: I know that a good deal of tyranny and chaos has undoubtedly existed within the Christian tradition. But I remain convinced that that same tradition enshrines the resources we need if we are to refresh our political discourse, never mind our practice.) Only when we get our democracy in better working order will the rule of law again be felt as an appropriate framework for civil life rather than an arbitrary and potentially unjust imposition.

Analysis: history and postmodernity

I regard it as a hopeful sign that we are today being more explicit than we were a generation ago about the ambiguous nature of the European and American Enlightenment. Many have highlighted the way in which our perceptions of that many-sided moment and movement have themselves turned into carefully constructed myths, such as that of the great victory of reason and science over ignorance and tyrannical tradition. It is no longer possible simply to say, 'We are the children of the Enlightenment, therefore we must think and behave thus and so.' Any movement that gave us the guillotine as one of its first fruits ('Look! A nice, clean and efficient way to kill your political opponents!') and the Gulag as one of its finest cannot simply be affirmed as it stands. This is not, of course, to suggest that we unthinkingly embrace a postmodern, still less a pre-modern, viewpoint. To refer again to dentistry: I have no desire to have my teeth hacked about by a postmodern dentist. Or a pre-modern one, for that matter.

But the myths of the Enlightenment have given birth today to a worrying stand-off between an increasingly shrill secularism and an increasingly powerful fundamentalism, whether Christian, Muslim, Hindu or some other. In that stand-off, as with many such polarizations, any suggestions of a nuanced approach which redraws the map are rejected and vilified as straightforward capitulation to the other side. This reminds me of the moment in Shakespeare's *Julius Caesar* where Cinna the poet is mistaken for Cinna the conspirator; when the mistake is discovered, the mob goes ahead and lynches the poet anyway. Once the blood-lust is up, saying 'That isn't what I said' is met with a shrug of the shoulders.

This stand-off between secularism and fundamentalism takes many forms. We have, perhaps most obviously, the fresh attack on religious belief launched in the name of empirical science by Richard Dawkins, the late Christopher Hitchens, Sam Harris and others. I say 'in the name of', but actually the rhetoric used by those three and others goes way beyond empirical science itself and into the realm of good old-fashioned mud-slinging. Just as the media refused to engage with what Archbishop Rowan actually said, so Dawkins and others refuse to engage with real theologians, not to mention real communities of faith that are making a vital difference at places where the world is in deep pain, a pain which the advances of science have often exacerbated (through weapons technology and the like) rather than alleviated. Just as European science in the nineteenth century was anything but politically neutral, but must be understood within the Enlightenment-based projects of imperial and technological expansion, leading inexorably to the First World War, so the present anti-religious scientific protests must be understood within the multivalent culture of late modernity. And if anyone supposes that that last sentence represents a Luddite anti-scientific protest, that merely shows how deeply the spurious stand-off between two polarized positions has gone into our thinking. All this, however, is a subject for another time.

More important for our present purposes are the tricky interfaces I've highlighted between faith and public life. We need, briefly, to set them in historical context.

It has often been pointed out that whereas in the first half of the eighteenth century it was possible to argue that thoughtful people could study the natural order and come to the conclusion that the Christian faith was true, by the second half of the same century this move had suffered a severe blow. The crucial change came as a result of the Lisbon earthquake of 1 November 1755. Before then, wise scholars like one of my famous Durham predecessors, Bishop Joseph Butler, could argue step by step for some kind of 'natural theology'. Butler died in 1752, and the earthquake three years later shook European culture just as much as it had shaken Lisbon itself. Suddenly it was not so obvious that a good and wise God was in charge of the world. This gave fresh ammunition to those who had been exploring Deism rather than Christian faith: God was removed from the natural world, and so could not be blamed for its horrors. Religion then became a matter of private spirituality in the present and an escapist heaven in the future. (Theologians will note that prior to this many had embraced a postmillennial vision of a coming earthly Utopia, and that it was after this that the premillennial, dualistic vision of Armageddon and 'rapture' began to be popular. This is discussed, though not I think always understood, in the interesting but to my mind flawed first chapter of John Gray's book *Black Mass: Apocalyptic religion and the death of utopia* (London: Penguin, 2008).)

But the shift to Deism was not just a matter of solving a tricky metaphysical problem, namely the involvement of the supposedly good creator with the apparent arbitrary violence of the present creation. It correlated exactly with the politics of the day. Remove God from involvement in the world, and we can then carve up the world without interference. The clergy are there to tell people how to go to heaven, not to lecture them about slavery or profit margins or manufacturing techniques. Many today still assume that position. The default mode for much public discourse today is to see any involvement of God within the public world as a straightforward category mistake. Often those who repeat this idea seem to be unaware of the cultural and historical conditioning of this perspective, let alone just how bizarre, in terms of the wider world, a view like this actually is. Nor are they aware, it seems, of how much manifest wickedness has been perpetrated because of it.

The Enlightenment precipitated several attempts at addressing the question of God in public. We here glance at four. To begin with, the United States enshrined a complete and formal separation of church and state, to which appeal is constantly made today, for instance in the debates about prayer in schools and about the propriety of printing 'In God We Trust' on dollar bills. (When I go to the USA I astonish people when I speak about the way in which British churches are heavily involved in the public education system.) This didn't at all mean the suppression of the churches, but rather the insistence that the churches should not deal in politics. American preachers who insist on talking about current political issues have been warned that their churches might lose their charitable status. However, since Ronald Reagan made 'God Bless America' his campaign song, it has become increasingly clear that you can't keep faith and politics separate in the United States. For many in that country the question now is how to hold them together. The last few years have not made this any easier.

The second example, France, is superficially similar. France had a revolution around the same time that America did, but they were quite different underneath. The American Revolution was more anti-British than anti-clerical; insofar as it had an anti-clerical element, the real target was the bishops who had been sent over by George III. The French Revolution, however, had an explicit anti-clerical core. One of its watchwords was Voltaire's famous slogan against the Roman Catholic Church: *Écrasez l'infame!* ('Wipe out the disgrace!'). Thus the American settlement instantiated a post-Protestant, or indeed post-Anglican, Deism; the French one, a post-Catholic atheism. The perception in France of Catholicism as a heavy-handed system, determined to dominate the whole society, generated by way of reaction an overt and insistent secularism. From that point of view, the republic which resulted from the revolution is held in theory to be already basically perfect. This makes it difficult to criticize the way it actually works, let alone to propose significant alterations. Even to think like that would question the foundation on which the whole society stands. The Enlightenment-driven privatization of religion and faith has thus taken very different forms in America and France.

Third, there is the straightforward replacement of religion by the state, as in the old Soviet Union. The idea of an atheist state didn't just mean, of course, that the leading communists happened not to believe in God. It meant, rather, that the role of God within the entire system was actually taken by the state, more particularly by the Party. This is *vox populi vox Dei* with the lid off – or rather with the lid clamped firmly down on the system, so that whatever is deemed to be good for the state or the Party is deemed to possess the kind of self-evident rightness which no-one in their right mind would challenge or question. The answer to God in public is both that there is no God as such and also that the state has become divine.

Fourth – this will surprise some, but I am quite clear that it belongs on the same map – there is the present English system which we still call the Established Church. (I speak only of England. There are different stories to tell in Scotland, Wales and Ireland.) The present system goes back to the sixteenth-century Reformation, with one major rupture in the mid-seventeenth century. But the present mode and working of the Establishment owes just as much to its Enlightenment reshaping as it does to its Reformation origins. Many people today don't understand this, since they imagine that Establishment makes the church simply a branch of the state, or indeed vice versa. Some who argue against the system of Establishment do so on the grounds that it gives the church too much power in the state; others, on the grounds that it gives the state too much power over the church. These cannot both be true. In fact, neither is. But the realignment of power within England in the late eighteenth and early nineteenth century, producing parliamentary democracy and constitutional monarchy as we know them today, has radically changed the mood and flavour of Establishment from anything that would have been recognized in, say, the 1660s, let alone the 1580s. Though at some levels church and state in England remain confusingly intertwined, in many other ways they are just as carefully distinguished as in the USA, albeit by steady implicit secularization rather than by sudden constitutional pronouncement. For the record, the place both of the free churches and of the Roman Catholic Church within England is also, by reflex as it were, to be understood within the same cultural setting. This then generates further confusions. Granted that since the Enlightenment people regularly understand 'religion' to be, by definition, something which people do in private, away from public life, this then frames the perceptions of, and debates about, the so-called 'other faiths'. This makes it almost impossible for people even to conceive the kind of worldviews represented by, say, classic Judaism and Islam, let alone to understand what it might mean for their adherents to belong to, or to flourish within, the England of today.

So much for a very brief analysis of where we are and how we've got there. I now have a threefold proposal. (i) The confusions we have observed are indications of an increasing instability which has generated the present stand-off between secularism and fundamentalism, as the two sides in the Deist divide now perceive themselves as fighting for their lives against a suddenly awakened foe. (ii) The chilly winds of postmodernity, blowing their deconstructive gales through the entire eighteenth-century settlement, are threatening the Enlightenment systems themselves and the secularism and fundamentalism to which they often seem reduced. (iii) Out of this postmodern moment there might yet emerge, as Archbishop Rowan suggested, new paths towards a wise and civil society in which the genuine values for which the Enlightenment was striving can be preserved and enhanced while the excesses to which it has given rise can be avoided. I take these in order.

Secularism and fundamentalism

Nobody familiar with England or the USA, to look no further, could doubt that the eighteenth-century settlement has become increasingly unstable. This is not just because of the large-scale migrations of people who hold to very different religions. It is, rather, that the neat separation of religion and culture, church and state, faith and public life, upon which the settlement was predicated simply isn't true to religion, church and faith on the one hand or to culture, state and public life on the other. Keeping them apart is artificial and sometimes impossible. I remember watching with fascination after the attacks of September 11, 2001 as George Bush led a great service in Washington National Cathedral: what on earth did that mean, granted the US Constitution? The British tableaux of civil religion often have the same feel. When the militant left-wing secularist Jeremy Corbyn became Leader of the Opposition in 2015, people watched the television with ironic interest as he wore a red poppy for the Remembrance Day service, and even appeared to be singing the hymn from memory.

Scenes like that remind me of those moments in older romantic films when the hero and heroine, who weren't supposed to be entangled with one another, bump into one another by accident and find themselves in an unintended kiss or clinch. They then stare at each other with awkward embarrassment. What was that all about? Does it mean we belong together in some way? What will our own partners – the secularist myth on the one hand, the fundamentalist dream on the other – have to say about it when they find out? To be sure, the secularist, looking on, is furious at the unfaithfulness of the state, and the fundamentalist at the apparent compromise of the church. The movie is heading for further complications.

Meanwhile, and more hopefully, there are many places in the UK in which everyone takes for granted a cheerful cooperation of church and state, not just the Anglican Church either, on a hundred matters of public life. The church is perceived as an intelligent and valued partner in housing, education, the care of the elderly, the plight of the hill farmers, the challenge of asylum-seekers, and much besides. Likewise, in the USA, many churches are extremely active in areas which the state, in its hands-off anti-communist mode, has been reluctant to touch, particularly the provision of help for those who can't afford it. The lines are (in other words) increasingly blurred, and the implicit settlement in which 'God into Public Won't Go' is more and more obviously called into question. This has merely increased the widespread sense that the Enlightenment split no longer corresponds to reality – which in turn increases the fury of the secularists whose cherished rumour of the complete demise of religion turns out to be exaggerated and premature. They then behave like a maverick doctor faced with the apparent recovery of the patient he had pronounced terminally ill. He turns to euthanasia to justify his original diagnosis.

Deconstructing modernity

All this, second, is part of the postmodern revolution which deconstructs more or less everything about the eighteenth-century Western settlement. Technology has brought nightmares as well as blessings. Post-Enlightenment empire has enslaved more millions than it has liberated, has brought wealth to the few and poverty to the many. Western justice favours those in power, not only incidentally but structurally. And the banishing of religion to the margins of life has been found sterile, denying something as basic to being human as music or falling in love. As I have argued elsewhere, we all know we should do justice but we are puzzled at how difficult it is; we all want spirituality but we aren't sure where to find it; we all love beauty but we can't understand why; we know we are made for relationship with one another but we've forgotten how to get it right. In the same way, we all know that freedom matters, but we can't agree on what it really is or how to facilitate it for ourselves or for others. And we know that there is a difference between straight thinking and crooked, between genuine reasoning and mere rationalization, but we find it hard to attain the former and avoid the latter. All these puzzles have cast doubt on the simple, grand modernist dream.

We have therefore deconstructed the big stories by which our society has lived for two hundred years, perceiving them as dehumanizing, serving the interests of a powerful elite. This postmodern mood has called everything into question, including Reason itself. That in turn is why, though in many ways our media love to feed us with the sterile nostrums of late modernity, their methods are relentlessly postmodern: spin and smear, innuendo and multiple misrepresentation. This is an exciting but dangerous time. We cannot take anything for granted as we try to find our way forward in the twenty-first century.

Proposal: God, kingdom and hope

In this complex situation we need to listen again for the rumour of other possibilities. Like St Paul in Athens, the church must offer both a critical analysis of the swirling currents of thought and life and a fresh possibility, a new fixed point, from which one might work outwards to fresh agendas. And that means talking about the kingdom of God.

The fate of this overused slogan illustrates nicely the problem we face. The phrase 'kingdom of God' meant to some in the first century, and has meant from time to time since, the establishment of a hands-on theocracy in which God himself would step in and direct the course of affairs. Since few have thought that the world's creator would be visibly present to do this, the scheme usually meant the delegation of the kingdom to some favoured earthly representative: a tyranny, in other words, of God's spokesmen (they were usually men). So strong was this vision among first-century Jews that they embarked on crazy wars with the Romans until, having been beaten again and again, some declared (in the mid-second century) that they should abandon the hope of the kingdom and instead 'take upon themselves the yoke of Torah': in other words, they should settle for private study and the keeping of their own law, while being content to live under whichever empire happened to be in power. That is the line which most Jews have taken to this day, negotiating in generation after generation that settlement under pagan law which seemed best at the time, always aware that the pagans might make demands on their consciences, and after that on their lives. That represented, in the second century, a middle position between the Christians, who went on insisting that Jesus was in fact the world's true Lord (and often died for it), and the Gnostics, who insisted that the 'kingdom' was a purely spiritual sphere into which one could escape, thus avoiding the political question altogether. It represented in the twentieth century a terrible and cruel dilemma and disaster from which the conscience of Europe has yet to recover.

So what does 'kingdom of God' actually mean in early Christian usage? Already by late in the second century the phrase was used in what many suppose to be its primary or even its only meaning: the realm of 'heaven', a disembodied post-mortem existence with no connection whatever to public or political life. Tracking the shift from its original meaning (God becoming king within the real world) to this very different position is not my present purpose. But we should be clear, as I have argued extensively elsewhere (notably in *Surprised by Hope*), that the first-century Christians, following Jesus himself, insisted as does the Lord's Prayer on God's kingdom coming 'on earth as in heaven'. 'All authority in heaven *and on earth* has been given to me,' declares the risen Jesus at the end of Matthew's gospel (28.18). That is the basis on which he then commissions his disciples for their worldwide mission. As recent New Testament studies have emphasized, here and elsewhere the early Christians turn out to have embraced what we today would call, if not exactly a political vision, a vision with direct political consequences. To put it crudely and perhaps oversimply, Jesus is Lord, therefore Caesar isn't.

The vision of the ultimate future which accompanies this is not, as so often imagined, a dream of an other-worldly sphere, away from space, time and matter altogether. The older idea that the early Christians expected the imminent end of the space-time universe is itself a post-Enlightenment construct, a way of parking Jesus and his first followers in a safe place where they couldn't get out and disturb the ongoing Enlightenment project. No: the early Christians held to a vision of creation renewed and reordered, in which renewed humans (the word is 'resurrection', of course) will live in renewed bodies. And, most disturbing of all, the early Christians believed that this new state of affairs, this 'new creation' as they called it, had actually already begun, with the resurrection of Jesus himself.

Now obviously the early Christians knew that this belief was ridiculous, and they were routinely ridiculed for it. We must never slip into the silly Enlightenment idea that only with the rise of modern science do we know that dead people don't rise. Homer knew that. So did Plato, Pliny and everybody else. The Jews believed that people would be raised at the end of time; the Christians agreed, but said that one person had been raised in anticipation of this event, and that he was therefore the world's true Lord. God in public, indeed: the scandal of the resurrection has never been merely that it breaks the laws of nature so called, but that it breaks into the *political* order, the world of societies and laws and government. It insists that a new world has begun: that the puzzles and pains of the old one can not only be understood, but creatively and healingly addressed, by working at them from within the new one.

The proof of the pudding remains in the eating. The communities that sprang up under the lordship of this strange figure called Jesus were themselves the living evidence of a God at work in the public domain, generating a new kind of justice, of rationality, of spirituality, of beauty, of relationship, of freedom. The life which these communities exemplified created a head-on challenge to actual regimes, which was why the church was so viciously persecuted for nearly three centuries. They also provided an alternative society, to which people were drawn in increasing numbers, so that the church went on growing despite the persecution. This explains why standard Enlightenment discourse includes a list of the church's obvious failings – crusades, inquisitions and the like – and a strange silence about its massive achievements in health, education, the arts, and many other spheres.

From very early on, leading Christian thinkers realized that the question of 'God in public' was vital and central, and they answered it in various ways. (One of the extraordinary triumphs of the Enlightenment has been to suggest that there could be no such thing as 'Christian political theology', since by late eighteenth-century standards such a thing would be a category mistake. There was in fact a massive and serious tradition from the first century, with the writings of the gospels and of Paul, through to the eighteenth century, with which we are only just now starting to reconnect, perhaps just in time.) John Gray's book *Black Mass* highlights what he calls the would-be Christian utopianism of Bush and Blair. In fact, the movements of thought he analyses are a parody, a caricature, of a reality. The reality itself is both more interesting and more potentially fruitful.

The first thing to be said about a Christian political theology is that it envisages God working through human beings to bring order and justice to the world. The Judaeo-Christian tradition insists that humans are made in God's image. They are called, not just to reflect God back to God, but to reflect God into God's world. They are called, that is, to be *stewards of creation*. The Bible applies this notion directly to the idea of political authority. Whether or not particular rulers consciously acknowledge the creator God, they are given the responsibility of bringing God's wise order to human society and indeed to the whole created world. Within this, they can be *rulers*, not just 'leaders', because there is such a thing as wise order, the giving of a framework to things, not just the chance to take people forward into new experiences and possibilities. The post-Enlightenment suspicion of the very word 'rulers', and its preference for 'leaders' as though the former automatically entailed tyranny, has its sting drawn by the multiple imagery, throughout the Judaeo-Christian scriptures, of tending the garden, looking after the flock of sheep, dressing the vine, and so on. A shepherd who tyrannizes the flock soon won't have any sheep left. Gardeners who uproot plants and put up concrete buildings instead have stopped being gardeners and have become something else.

The trouble is, of course, that at the point where ancient theology and contemporary philosophy meet we find a new awareness of the problem of evil. If we hadn't noticed it before – if, for instance, we thought we in the West had 'evil' solved in principle until September 11, 2001 came along and spoiled it all – that merely demonstrated how naive we were being (on this, see my *Evil and the Justice of God*). The ancient doctrine of original sin, and the postmodern insistence that all our great stories are designed to boost someone's power and prestige, converge at this point. Those who are called to rule, by whatever means they come to that status, are instantly tempted to exercise that power for their own benefit. The idea that any earthly ruler, even someone intensely devout in private life, can exercise a pure authority, and go about ridding the world of evil, always was a crazy dream, whether it be in the Crusades of the Middle Ages or in those of the early twenty-first century. What has happened is that, in the post-Enlightenment split-level reality, the utopian dreams have been inspired not by the Christian message but by the Enlightenment's self-fulfilling prophecies of its own automatic superiority over the rest of the world, qualifying the enlightened West to be the world's police officer – at the same time, conveniently, as technology has enabled it to be the world's only superpower. Here the Enlightenment has shown at last that it knows it really is based on the moral foundation of the Judaeo-Christian heritage, the calling to bring justice and mercy to the world. But because it denies the truth which lies at the very heart of that heritage, that is, the message of and about Jesus himself, it has twisted that tradition into a horrible parody.

How then can that hidden truth inform our thinking about God in public? How can we glimpse new hope within the political and legal sphere coming from that unlikely place, the Christian vision which is so often thought of as being 'merely' about faith and spirituality, and thus not relevant to the wider world?

The answer lies in the notions of service and suffering. These stand in the Jewish scriptures as the sign that the people who bear witness to the creator God will find themselves on a different trajectory from the world which insists on going its own way. That was always the case. When the Children of Israel were coming out of Egypt, they were warned that they had to live a life different from the customs of both Egypt, from which they had escaped, and Canaan, to which they were going. Bit by painful bit, ancient Israelite poets and prophets wrestled with the strange possibility of the kingdoms of the world becoming the kingdom of God, and found themselves ground between those upper and nether millstones. And it is out of that essentially Jewish vision of a people bearing witness to a different way of being human, serving God and serving God's world, that the first Christians, following the hints of Jesus himself, interpreted his horrible death not simply as a tragedy (though it was that as well) but as the climax of his kingdom-announcement. They saw his death as the point at which all that suffering came rushing together, as Israel's Messiah was executed by the pagan powers outside the walls of his own capital city. Evil did its worst to Jesus, and he took it and exhausted its power. And that, too, only made the sense it did because the Christians dared to believe, from exceedingly early on, that in that event they had witnessed, all unknowing, 'God in public', God stripped naked, God shamed and beaten, God ruling the world from the cross with the power, not of military might, but of love.

This dream is completely off the radar screen for much of our contemporary culture, not least because the churches have themselves hushed it up. The Western churches have colluded so effectively with the split-level world of the Enlightenment that the cross is reduced to the celestial mechanism whereby we escape the wicked world of sin rather than the coming of God into the public world to establish his kingdom. One of the reasons (not the only one) why many church people were outraged at what the media suggested that Rowan Williams had been saying is that many Western Christians have never asked themselves what Jesus meant when he taught us to pray that God's kingdom would come on earth as in heaven. But the original vision of the crucified Jesus will in fact deconstruct the angry rant of the fundamentalist, even as it will confront the scorn of the secularist. The cross will not let the fundamentalist corrupt the message into self-serving power, just as it will not let the secularist get away with the standard critique of dangerous religion. The cross is at the heart of a redefinition of the word 'God' itself which will open up new possibilities for what it might mean to think of 'God in public'.

Working out in practice what this might mean has never been easy – to put it mildly. Church history is littered with ghastly mistakes, as emperors and popes have translated the kingdom of God too readily into the kingdoms of their own systems, eliminating both the service and the suffering. But with Jesus the new order has been inaugurated, and political power – anybody's political power – can now be seen as the anticipation of the rescuing, restorative justice by which the living creator God will one day put the whole world to rights. *And that contextualizes all political and legal work in the present*, and moreover bequeaths to the church the task of holding governments of whatever sort to account. The early church, like the ancient Jews, wasn't particularly concerned with how governments and rulers came to power. They were extremely concerned to hold up a mirror to them and show how they were doing in terms of the yardstick of the restorative justice of God himself.

The Enlightenment world gets that the other way round: we are obsessed with how people come to power, and then, provided a vote, an election, has taken place, we suppose that all that follows is automatically legitimated. (I have heard serious Americans declare that, because George Bush was validly elected – some, of course, have questioned that as well – nobody, certainly no Christian, had any right to object to his bombing Iraq.) No: the political and legal vision of 'God in public' by which the early Christians lived involved the simultaneous *affirmation* of the *authority* of rulers and *critique* of what they actually *did* – a balance which the modern Western world has found it hard to maintain. This leads to the postmodern collapse, where all we have is critique and no affirmation at all, and the new secularist would-be tyranny, where whatever the government decrees must be instantly binding on all subjects, even if it squashes their consciences out of shape.

So the starting-point for a Christian political theology must be that the creator God desires to work through human beings to bring his wise, healing stewardship to the world, whether or not those humans explicitly acknowledge his presence, love or wisdom. Second, though, and much more briefly, this vision must not stop with a small number of elite rulers. That rule must be shared, all the way through the system: the restoration of genuine responsible humanness must be the method as well as the goal. And that means the sharing of power; which means, in the last analysis, some form of democracy. Here again we glimpse the truth that the Enlightenment was actually quite a close-up Christian heresy. It was attempting to gain the great prize of a genuinely Christian vision of a humane and humanizing society, but without the Christian faith to back it up. It grasped instead at the dream of its own glory, claiming to be the climax of history through which everything would be healed. But in doing so it pushed the real climax of history, the God-in-Public moment of Jesus and his death and resurrection, into the long-range backdrop for a 'religion' whose street-level energy had been drained off into a detached spirituality.

We can sum all this up as follows. First, with Jesus God's rule has been inaugurated, and present rulers must be held to account, in the light not of some abstract or ancient ideal but of the coming moment when God will himself put all things to rights. Second, this must work out in the present in ways that are themselves ennobling, drawing more and more people up into their full human stature as part of the decision-making process. Third, and finally, the signs of this 'kingdom' will be a society at work to rescue and heal, to reorder priorities so that the weakest are defended and the strongest prevented from pride and power. It is wonderfully ironic that inside the front cover of the *New Statesman* which carried the original set of articles on 'God in Public', there was an advertisement for the Salvation Army, under the heading 'Belief in Action'. The actions in question, I need hardly add, were not dropping bombs or bullying minorities, but helping the homeless, befriending the endangered young, and healing drug addicts. That is not the only thing that 'God in public' looks like from a Christian point of view, but it stands near the centre of that vision. It is a sign of hope, hope that refuses to die – or, if it does, insists on rising again soon afterwards.

Conclusion: public God, public agenda

Some brief remarks in conclusion, to relate all this to current controversies. To begin with, the stand-off between secularism and fundamentalism. To quote again the words of the American Jim Wallis, 'the right gets it wrong and the left doesn't get it'. The church is called in every generation to be a community, a public community, working with all who will collaborate for the public good, in the belief that God *will* one day put all things to rights, that he *has already done so* in Jesus, and that the human calling here and now is to order our lives and our societies in such a way that they draw energy from the latter and genuinely anticipate the former. If the church had been doing that the last two hundred years – and it is two hundred years since Wilberforce and his friends got the slave trade abolished in Britain and its colonies – we would be having a very different debate today. Ironically, it is because the church has so often shirked its public role, regularly justifying that withdrawal by using the language of 'heaven' but filling it with Enlightenment dualism, that our present puzzles about the Establishment of the church have taken the shape they have.

'Establishment' is a way of recognizing that England is still in theory a Christian country, both in the sense that our history and culture have been decisively shaped by the Christian faith and life and in the sense that, at the 2011 census, 59 per cent of the population called themselves 'Christian'. This means that the 'Established' Church has a special responsibility to take thought for, and speak up for, the small minorities, and to ensure that they are not squashed between an unthinking church and an uncaring secular state. Hence Rowan Williams' perfectly proper concern for the particular sensitivities of Muslims, as indeed of Jews and others. And most Church of England leaders would insist today that if some way could be found to share our 'Established' status with our great sister churches, we would be delighted. But let's not fool ourselves. To give up 'Establishment' now would be to collude with that secularism which postmodernity has cheerfully and rightly deconstructed. Rather, the challenge ought to be to make it work for the benefit of the whole society. To aim at that would be to work with the grain both of the Christian gospel itself and of the deep roots of our own society and traditions.

In particular, we need to recapture that which the Enlightenment highlighted but which has been lost in the world of postmodernity and spin-doctors: the emphasis on Reason in our thinking and our public discourse. Reason is correlated with Trust. When you don't really trust your conversation partner to be thinking things through in a reasoned manner, you cut in with smear and innuendo. And when you don't quite trust *yourself* to think things out either, you resort to spin and slogans. That double lack of trust correlates directly, if ironically, with the Enlightenment's insistence on separating God from the public world. Many politicians, and many in the media, hope to control what people think and do; if they can't, they will rubbish them instead. Trusting people is an altogether different way of proceeding, and it needs different back-up mechanisms. Wise as serpents, said Jesus, and innocent as doves. Perhaps part of the unintended consequence of the postmodern revolution is to show that if Reason is to do what it says on the tin we may after all need to reckon with God in public. And when that happens we need wise Christian voices at the table, and for that matter wise Jewish and Muslim voices and many others beside, voices neither strident nor fundamentalist, voices both humble and clear: the voices, not of those with instant answers, but of those with a fresh grasp of God's truth, whose word will carry conviction because it appeals, like Paul in Athens with the altar to the unknown God, to things which everybody half knows but many try to suppress.

Within that project, finally, there is a massive challenge to our contemporary democratic institutions. The way successive governments in the UK have tinkered with constitutional reform, playing with long-established structures as though they were a set of toy soldiers, pays no attention to the checks and balances in the old system, and lacks any kind of guiding vision except the vague one that more voting is probably a good thing, presumably because the Enlightenment said so. I am all in favour of voting, for the reasons I have already explained. But there must also be structural means of holding executives and governments to account, which still seems extremely difficult to do, whether in broad outlines or in specific details. One of the urgent tasks of the church today might be to help give an account of our democratic structures, how they are failing in their tasks, and how they might be reformed to address them better. That would take us into other areas, of course, not least the complexities of a Europe where all the ideological battles I've been describing are magnified and multiplied. But the church should not simply be sitting on the sidelines trying to protect an anachronistic privilege. If those of us who belong to the church believe what we say, we should be helping give a lead in figuring out what it means in tomorrow's world to do God in Public, and encouraging our fellow citizens, not least other households of faith, into that wise, reasoned and civil discourse. This, and this alone, will get us where we need to go. This, and this alone, will keep us on track as we make the journey into the strange, dangerous but also hopeful world of post-postmodernity.

6

God, power and human flourishing

I vividly remember an evening in my schooldays when a shock-wave went through the school community, even as it was echoing through the global community. We were just coming out of a concert that night when the rumour went round that President Kennedy had been shot dead in Dallas. We didn't know what it would mean, but we knew it was a defining moment. Since then we have lived through some other great defining moments, and it's impossible to guess what they will mean in the longer term. But we can have a stab at sketching some of the issues that will be swirling around us as we feel our way forward into this new and startling set of possibilities.

In particular, I want to ask the question of where, if anywhere, God might belong in and among it all. We all face a particular challenge: are we going to be bystanders, or are we going to learn the grammar of the subject so that we can join in intelligently and creatively?

To help get started on the latter option, I offer some reflections on power and money. Power and money are two of the great driving interests in all human affairs ancient, modern and postmodern. We need to think about the way they are performing in the world of today and tomorrow. But first, a word about a word, the puzzling little word 'God' itself.

God and the gods

If you walk down the street and ask the first person you meet, 'Do you believe in God?', the chances are that the answer you get, in Europe and America at least, will assume one particular meaning for the word 'God'. Most people in the UK still think of 'God' as an old man up in the sky, who may or may not have made the world, and is supposed to be running it efficiently, but isn't doing a very good job of it. As Woody Allen said, 'I believe in God; it's just that he seems to be a bit of an underachiever.' This God is supposed to have a set of rules for how human beings behave, and he is rumoured to be planning some kind of final examination in which we'll all be tested on how well we've done – though according to other variations it's done on a continuous assessment basis, which is in fact equally troubling. This God is supposed to have something to do with Jesus of Nazareth, though quite what it's hard to say. Some people seem to think this God steps into the world from time to time to perform remarkable stunts to remind us he's still around, and then seems to disappear again.

That, as I say, is the probable picture people will have in their minds if you ask whether they believe in God. Many of those people will be practising Christians, who assume that this is the God they are supposed to believe in, and who somehow fit their knowledge and love and worship of Jesus himself into this picture. Equally, there are many atheists who, when you ask them which God it is they don't believe in, describe one like that. The picture is of God as a grumpy old despot, and not even a very efficient one at that. I was recently reading a book on modern Italy in which the writer pointed out one particular irony: Mussolini was a tyrant with absolute power – in a country where nobody obeys the laws anyway. Some people think God is a bit like that. He's supposed to be running the show, and we may not much like that idea, but we still wish he'd get it right and not allow tsunamis, earthquakes or famines – or genocides or child-abuse . . .

This picture of God does not, in fact, have very much to do with the specifically *Christian* understanding. Nor, for that matter, does a very different picture which you also meet from time to time: the pantheist dream that God and the world are more or less the same thing. For the pantheist, the natural forces within the world, and within each one of us, are somehow themselves divine. The point then is not to obey (or disobey!) a distant God, but to get in touch and in tune with the divine force inside ourselves. Many philosophies have gone that route, but it's just as problematic as the picture of the old man up in the sky. In particular, of course, it offers no solution to the problem of evil: if God and the world are pretty much the same thing, and if you don't like the way the world is, there is nowhere to hide.

These two pictures of God – the distant, detached, inefficient deity on the one hand, and the kind of 'soul of the world' on the other –

correspond more or less to the ancient philosophies of Epicureanism and Stoicism. And in the middle there have always been people who say that God, or the gods, may well exist, but we can't be sure, so it's best to keep some form of religion going just in case. That is a typically English position (alas, sometimes a typically Anglican one!). Its ancient counterpart was the so-called Academic viewpoint. I mention these ancient philosophies to make the point that the subject of theology – what you think about God, or the gods, and the world, and how they relate or don't relate to one another – has a recognizable shape. It is quite easy to learn this shape, even though it then takes a lifetime to work out in detail; and if you don't learn this shape you will not be able to think clearly about why people order their lives and societies in the ways they do.

This is so particularly when we factor in the very different belief of mainline Christian faith. The early Christians were quite clear that you couldn't start with an existing picture of God and then simply fit Jesus into it. You had to start with Jesus and work out from there. And when they did that – within the classic ancient Jewish viewpoint, naturally – they found that they had some common ground with the ancient philosophers, but that they were also bound to issue strong challenges to them. And on this basis they went out, looked the world in the eye – the world of power, money and sex, then as now – and announced that Jesus was its rightful Lord, and that following him was the way to a genuinely human existence at last, corporate and individual. Thus they managed, at a stroke, to poke in the eye most of the vested interests of the ancient world – which was of course why they were so fiercely persecuted. But they established a way of life which more and more people found utterly compelling, creative and consoling, despite the surrounding hostility. And my question in this chapter can be reframed in these terms: supposing we think of *this* God, and ask what it would mean, as it were, to 'do God in public' in our strange and dangerous new century. What might that look like?

God and power in tomorrow's world

I begin with power – appropriately enough, since this chapter was first given as a lecture in the week when Barack Obama was elected as President of the United States, giving him overnight more real power than any other human on the planet. To reflect on power we need to think for a moment of the story of the last two centuries in the Western world, and what has happened to that story. The essentially Epicurean vision of God, or the gods, a long way away from the world, unconcerned and uninvolved, generates the standard view, which many in our country to this day assume is the only possible one, that God and human power have nothing to do with one another. And this, as I have said, was one of the driving forces of modern democracy. If God is kicked upstairs, as happened explicitly in France and America, then those who claim automatic divine legitimation, like monarchs, must themselves be removed from the equation, and those who claim to speak for God, like clergy, must be told to stick to spirituality and other-worldly salvation. An earlier generation might have said *vox populi vox Dei* ('The voice of the people is the voice of God'); but the revolutionaries of the eighteenth century decided that *vox populi* was enough as it stood, and would have to carry the whole weight of decision-making. God either wasn't around or wasn't interested. We had to sort everything out for ourselves. The political process would then continue, as in Epicurean philosophy the material world developed, under an automatic and self-generated process of evolution. This is what some thinkers have referred to as 'the biopolitical', a political process which moves along under its own steam like natural selection in biology.

Watch how that view then slides in two directions, both of which have contributed massively to the problems of the twentieth and now the twenty-first centuries. On the one hand, those who really did get rid of God altogether created a vacuum, and the state and its mechanisms grew to fill it. The regimes of China and the old Soviet Union were officially 'atheist', not just because people happened not to believe in God, but because *there was no room for God in the system*. The state had grown to fill the gap. The very rumour of God – any god! – was therefore deeply subversive. Alternatively, on the other hand, the vacuum could be filled by invoking a very different sort of god, the god or gods present within the natural world, the deep forces of blood and race and land, summoned up sometimes in an explicit throwback to earlier pagan beliefs, and generating what one can only call the theologically driven totalitarianism of the master race, the fatherland, the Leader who bears a disturbing resemblance to Nietzsche's Superman. Let's not fool ourselves. Theology matters. Harold Wilson, who became Prime Minister to great excitement and acclaim while I was a schoolboy, used the word 'theology' in a contemptuous fashion, to mean 'irrelevant theory'. But theologies are things to live for, and indeed to die for. It was theology, albeit deeply distorted theology, that caused a lot of people to die in the course of the last century or so.

The difficulty we then face is that it won't do to say, 'Well, that was wicked religious totalitarianism, but because we've got Western secular democracy we're all right, and all we need to do is to have more of it around the world.' Politicians when elected to office often declare how much they value the democratic system; if they say that after failing to be elected, they do so through clenched teeth! And we should never forget that democracies, all the way back to ancient Athens, have often voted in large majorities for ideals and actions which within a few years have been seen to be unwise and disastrous.

What's more, anyone who wants to get elected in today's democracies has to spend a large amount of money. When I first studied history as a schoolboy, we rather looked down on our benighted forefathers for holding 'elections' in which the local squire got a big barrel of beer and gave a party to all those who voted for him. Today we are more subtle and sophisticated, but it would be very short-sighted to suppose that all is well with our voting systems. In addition, it would be foolish to suppose, as most modern democracies seem to suppose, that gaining a majority at an election gives a person or a party an absolute and unchallengeable right to take any desired course of action. The ancient Greeks and Romans frequently used to put their public officials on trial once their term of office was over. It was no defence against charges of maladministration or corruption, or even well-meaning incompetence, to say that you had been voted in by a large majority in the first place. You were still accountable retrospectively as well. Today we've largely given that up, except in the case of really enormous scandals like Nixon's Watergate. *Vox populi* has spoken, in however peculiar a method and with whatever financial inducements, and our systems shrug their shoulders and say, 'Well, they got elected.' The only sanction then is not voting for them next time. But next time can seem a long way off; and, when it comes, there may be some pressing issue which pushes people to vote for one candidate even though that candidate may be misguided or downright dangerous on several other issues.

What might it mean, then, to speak of God in public in tomorrow's world of power, and to do so with the Christian God in mind rather than the distant Epicurean one, or the absent atheist one, or the blood-and-soil Stoic one? Let me just sketch, in five quick brushstrokes, the shape of such a thing.

Christ and power

To begin with, the God we see in Jesus Christ intends that there should be structures of human authority and the ordering of community life. Christians are not called to be anarchists, because the God we believe in is the creator, the God who brings order out of chaos. Anarchy sounds fine until you realize that it allows the bullies and the unscrupulous to prey on the weak and the vulnerable. Farmers would be quite happy not to have any walls around their fields, as long as there aren't any wolves out there ready to snatch the lambs. No; the New Testament is quite clear: God intends that there should be human power structures within the world.

Second, though, God remains sovereign over all human powers and authorities. This, too, is quite clear: human authorities are not divine, and they are called to account, ultimately, by God himself. Christians are not called to be tyrants, because the God we believe in is the power-sharing God who calls human beings to exercise responsibility under his overarching rule. The long memory of totalitarianism has made us all wary of suggesting that power structures are intended by God. The proper response is not to get rid of power structures but to insist that God remains sovereign over them.

Third, and most crucial and central, power has been redefined by and around Jesus Christ himself. This is a major strand in the New Testament. At one point (Mark 10.35–45), James and John, two of Jesus' less reticent disciples, suggest that they should sit at his right and left when he becomes King. They are already jockeying for position, not least, we may suppose, against the other obvious pair of brothers, Peter and Andrew. And Jesus tells them off with words which will, I hope, become increasingly familiar to Christians and others as well in tomorrow's generation. 'The rulers of the nations,' he says, 'lord it over their subjects, and their great ones exercise dominion over them. *But it's not going to be like that among you*: with you, anyone who wants to be great must become a servant, and anyone who wants to be first must be the slave of all.' And then, rubbing the point in but also widening it so that we see the full implications, he refers to his own forthcoming fate: 'because the Son of Man came not to be served but to serve, and to give his life as a ransom for many'. We have often pulled apart the two halves of that sentence: the political comment on the one hand and the saving death of Jesus Christ on the other. In tomorrow's world we will not be able to afford the luxury of that divided world. Somehow we must explore what it means that power itself has been redefined in, through and around Jesus Christ and his death and resurrection, *and* that salvation is not about escape *from* this world but about redemption *for* and *in* this world.

Let me just pause on this before giving you the fourth brushstroke. Some of this lesson is already enshrined in the language we use about those who govern us. We talk of 'civil *servants*', and of people working in the 'public *service*'. And, happily, plenty of those who use that language to describe themselves really do mean it, and act accordingly. But increasingly we have moved away from that, and towards the language of 'rulers', of 'leaders', and even of 'masters', often without reflecting on the subtle shifts that those words represent. This ambiguity lurks here and there within our democratic structures; because when we elect politicians we delegate to them the power to do the things we want them to do – to serve us, in other words. (This then generates a further puzzle, because those people must then decide not just what the voters wanted when they voted, but what is in fact in the best interests of them and everybody else – and these things may well not be the same, which is why among other things referendums can be very misleading.) But, as we all know, democracy can easily degenerate into something a very long way from this, and it would be a bold commentator who denied that that has happened and continues to happen in Western society today.

So the first three brushstrokes of a Christian redefinition of power go like this. First, God intends that there should be structures of authority; second, the authorities are not themselves divine but are accountable to God; third, power itself is redefined, in and around Jesus Christ, in terms of servanthood. This brings us now to the fourth, and crucial, point. The Christian believes that Jesus Christ will one day call the whole world to account, and put the whole world to rights, flooding the entire creation with his justice, his peace and his glory; *and the authorities are charged in the present time not only with implementing God's order in creation, but also anticipating God's final order, the bringing of justice, healing, peace and glory to God's world.* In other words, from the point of view of a serious Christian theology, you discern the task of human authorities not only in relation to the world as it is but in relation to the world as God intends to remake it.

This leads at once to the fifth and final brushstroke, which is a serious health warning. When you give this responsibility to human beings, whether it's President of the United States or the captain of a football team, they will always be tempted to use it for their own self-aggrandisement. Human authorities must therefore themselves always be held accountable. Human authorities are intended by God to be part of his solution to the problems of the world, anticipating his final putting-to-rights of all things; but they themselves are always in danger of becoming part of the problem. When that happens – when rulers give up being servants and become tyrants, which can happen just as much in a modern democracy as in an overtly monarchical system – you really do have a problem. One vital part of the church's task is then to remind the authorities what they are there for, and what they are not there for. The church must hold the rulers of the world to their responsibilities, speak clearly about their failures in relation to them, and – of course! – model its own life so that it is seen to be doing what it commends to others. This is, naturally, a large and complex task, but it is a necessary one.

The task of holding politicians to account is not normally conceived in these terms, either by our present politicians or by our present church leaders. The task is seen to be necessary, but we normally suppose that it falls to either the parliamentary opposition or the media and journalists. Both are sometimes effective and sometimes depressingly ineffective, with oppositions being unlikely to challenge governments when party policies happen to coincide and the media being notoriously fickle, sometimes corrupt, and often merely the mouthpiece of special interests. From the Christian point of view, both of these have a vital place. But the church retains the vocation to hold them all to account, however difficult or dangerous this may be, and however much, once more, the church must be visibly true in its own life to the standards it insists on for others.

A Christian analysis of human power offers a framework of thought and action which is significantly different from those which have undergirded our Western systems for the last two hundred or more years. Working together towards this goal is, I suggest, the best way of addressing the huge problems of our world, which are not solved simply by electing a new government or president. But what would it all mean in practice? Simply that clergy would preach challenging sermons and write occasional articles for the newspapers? Surely not. Let me suggest three quick examples of how it might work out in terms of 'doing God in public'.

Three examples

First, the church must remind those in power of their responsibilities. A few years ago, when I was in Rome for their Synod of Bishops, I received an email about an asylum-seeker from the Cameroon. This man, Anselme by name, inherited the position of tribal chief when his father died, but since this meant, for a start, marrying all his late father's wives, as a devout Christian he refused. The tribespeople tried to kill him, because their system required him to become chief, but he escaped to the UK. Here he settled and was working and trying to make a new life for himself. However, the authorities suddenly swooped on him, picked him up and tried to deport him, because, it seemed, they were trying to please the popular press by massaging the statistics on asylum-seekers, and picking on soft targets is easier than deporting genuinely dangerous people. Anselme was beaten up by the British security forces who were trying to take him on to the plane, but the other passengers that would have flown with him back to Cameroon stood up and refused to sit down until he was removed from the aircraft. He was brought back to custody in the UK. I and other church leaders wrote to the Prime Minister to complain in the strongest terms at this travesty of justice. The deportation order was stopped, and a fresh review ordered. Now in a sense you don't have to be a Christian to make this kind of point, but the fact that we were church leaders tells its own story, and our secular authorities, left to themselves, seemed either unwilling or unable to do anything. Sadly, the story did not have a happy ending. A few months later the authorities made another swoop, and this time succeeded in deporting Anselme to his dangerous fate.

Second, speaking of God means speaking out on behalf of the voiceless. Once again people are campaigning for what they call 'assisted dying' or even 'the right to die'. Hard cases make bad law, and there are always some desperate situations which wring your heart-strings. But the evidence from Holland on the one hand, and from the state of Oregon on the other, shows all too clearly that, once you allow people to opt for assisted suicide, all kinds of forces are unleashed, all kinds of subtle pressures come into play, which put already vulnerable people and families at enormous risk, not least psychological. I am proud that when this came up in the House of Lords the opposition was led by Archbishop Rowan Williams, partly on the grounds I've mentioned, but also on the grounds, on which the church joined forces with Jewish and Muslim leaders, that human life is a gift which it is not ours to take away. One could mention, in addition, that we in the UK are field leaders in palliative care, and that many whose lives might have been unbearable have found the way to a dignified natural death through the hospice move-ment, which was pioneered in this country on specifically Christian grounds. These are further signs of what it means to speak of God in tomorrow's world. Again, it was no surprise that some of those advocating a change in the law were angry with the Archbishop for 'foisting his religion' on to our supposedly modern, secular state.

My third example is a much harder one, because it's not something that's already happened but it is something which I believe urgently needs to happen. The United Nations has very little power when it comes to acting in times of political and social emergency. It has been kept weak not least because of the powerful interests that suspect they would themselves be in trouble if either the United Nations, or a truly International Criminal Court, were able to do more. But it is now clear that we need to do in international relations what we did in Britain early in the nineteenth century when the local constables, patrolmen and watchmen were joined together by Sir Robert Peel to form a nationwide police force which would be impartial, credible and effective. Naturally, powerful interests will oppose this idea, but the problem is that under our present systems, generated as they were within the prevailing Enlightenment Epicureanism, which is precisely a model of a distant authority that never intervenes, there is no means of articulating a vision of global reality within which a different way of doing things could be thought through. I suggest that it is high time that in speaking of God in tomorrow's world we work out what it would mean to set up structures of justice and peace that would be able to act, and act credibly, in today's Congo, in Darfur, in Syria and the rest of the Middle East, and in the many other places that will no doubt flare up in days to come. Speaking of the Christian God, in the ways I have set out, could form the platform for thinking through and working out fresh ways forward for the vast problems we currently face. I certainly don't see it happening any other way.

God and mammon

Let me now turn, much more briefly, to the other subject I promised. What might it mean to speak of God in a world dominated by mammon, by money?

What happened in the world of money in 2008 (the year in which this chapter was first presented as a lecture) was, to put it mildly, the economic equivalent of September 11, 2001. We never believed anything like the financial crash could happen, but looking back we can see not only why it did but also why we didn't see it coming. And just as it won't do to say, in relation to the events of September 11, that it was all because of some religious fanatics (so what we'd better do is to ban fanatics, or even bomb them, and then it'll all be all right), so it won't do to say that the financial crisis in all its extraordinary ramifications was because of a few greedy sub-prime traders, and that once we spank them the rest of the system can resume as normal. No. What is the alternative? What does it mean to think or speak of God in public in this sphere?

The Epicurean gods don't care what we do with our money, and they can't help us in the messes we create for ourselves. The pagan or Stoic gods encourage us to worship money, and there have been plenty of people doing that; you can always tell when an idol is being worshipped, because it demands sacrifices. Neither of these will do. If we are to speak of the Christian God in the public world of tomorrow, we have to speak of genuine human existence within God's good creation, and when we do that the Jewish, Christian and indeed Muslim traditions have some serious things to say to us about money. I just mention three.

First, it is fascinating that all these three traditions have, until recently, forbade the taking of interest on loans. Since our entire Western world is based on the principle of interest, indeed of compound interest, it is hard for us even to imagine a world without it. But the principle goes deep into the theology of creation and judgment, because the point of money, in any biblical theology, is that it is not a thing in itself, to be used as an end in itself, but is always directly related to goods and services. As soon as you get a second-order use of money (money used to make money, money used to bet on money), alarm bells ought to ring. I'm not sure we can prevent that, starting where we are right now, but we ought at least to be aware of it.

Second, though, any Christian is bound to note the enormous disparity between rich and poor in today's and tomorrow's world, and to recognize that this cannot reflect the reality of a good and wise creator. It will not do simply to say that we need a different tax structure, or more handouts. We must ask why the poor are poor, and address the underlying causes. Nor will it do to suggest a return to something like the communist proposal. That not only failed to provide Utopia, in its seventy-year trial in Russia and its satellites; it provided a massive and tyrannical Dystopia, taking millions of people to the grave with it.

As we address the underlying causes of poverty, third, we note that undeniably some of the poor are indeed poor because of their own folly or laziness or stupidity. But this undoubted truth has been used for far too long as an excuse on the part of the rich for carrying on regardless with selfish, greedy and completely unjust policies. I am speaking here on a global scale as well as locally. There are still several countries, not least in sub-Saharan Africa, which are massively indebted to Western countries and banks, and where entire populations are unable to spend money on health care, education and so on, because everything they make goes into paying the compound interest on the national debt. The usual excuse of the bankers – these people shouldn't have borrowed so much, it's their own fault, they are irresponsible, they have to learn that there's a day of reckoning, and so on – were completely blown out of the water by the events of 2008. That excuse can never again be made. The elite bankers were doing exactly the same thing. They were every bit as irresponsible as the craziest of third-world countries. But when they came whining to their governments (often flying in in their private planes to do so), the governments did for the very rich what they had refused to do for the very poor. Western governments, in fact, raised $700 billion to bail out 'the system'. It would cost a few hundred million, at the most, to bail out the very poor. If we did that, with proper safeguards *both* for the banks *and* for the countries involved, we might all be able to advance together.

To speak like this is not simply to advocate a piece of political prudence, though I believe it does that as well. It is to speak directly of the Christian God. This God, declares the Bible and the gospel, made the world to be ordered. He made human beings in his image and redeemed them to bear that image fully once more. He speaks again and again in scripture of his concern for the plight of the poor and his opposition to the arrogance of the rich. In Jesus Christ he came in person to take the weight of the world's evil on himself, so that the world might be rescued from evil and all that comes from it, and find its way to hope and human flourishing here and hereafter. St Paul, interestingly, uses the image of riches and poverty to describe this central fact of faith: he (Jesus) was rich, he says, yet for our sakes he became poor, so that we by his poverty might become rich (2 Corinthians 8.9). It is high time that we learned the new and difficult art of speaking of, and indeed acting for, this God in those parts of tomorrow's public world which right now are in serious confusion and in urgent need of fresh insight and wisdom.

God and human flourishing

I have so far spoken of God in relation to two of the big public issues we face in tomorrow's world. It may come as a surprise to some to think that the Christian faith has anything much to say about such things. I hope this has provided at least some food for thought. But I want to conclude this chapter by speaking more personally. The God revealed in Jesus Christ is not, of course, simply a God who sets up systems for running the world. The God we know in Jesus is as close to us as breath, and we need in our day to recapture the art of speaking of this God wisely, truthfully and fruitfully.

This is difficult for the reasons I've already mentioned. 'God' is usually thought to belong away upstairs somewhere, in the attic of our minds or hearts, to be met with perhaps in church but not very often, to be invoked at a wedding or funeral, but more as a way of labelling a puzzle on the edge of our experience than invoking a living reality at the centre of it. But my point in the present chapter has been this: only when we recapture something of the large-scale glory of who God actually is, only when we see, and start to put into practice, what it means to think of God's justice and mercy for the whole world, what it would look like to implement God's passion for the poor, and what it might mean to name God in some of the toughest decisions we face, can we escape the danger, in our personal lives, of treating God as a private hobby, perhaps even as a private saviour, who doesn't touch the rest of existence. We need to reckon with the strange presence and power of God, and renounce the idea that he is a long way away, or that he is only interested in our internal spirituality.

There is clearly an equal and opposite danger: that we might then so concentrate on the external world that we forget the internal. As that great scientist John Polkinghorne has been fond of saying, when you look through the finest microscope or the most powerful telescope, the most interesting object in the universe is still that which is two or three inches on this side of the lens. The human brain is extraordinary, making humans as a whole extraordinary; and Christians reaffirm the ancient Jewish belief that this is because we are made in God's image, made to reflect God out into his world and to do so, not as it were at a distance, but because the true God wants to make himself known to us, in us and through us. Somehow we have to recapture the art of speaking gladly and without embarrassment of this God. And of doing so in public.

We feel embarrassment at this. As a bishop I came to know only too well the hush which fell on a conversation if, at a dinner-table, someone asked me a direct question about God. The embarrassment comes because the Epicurean god, the Enlightenment God, doesn't belong downstairs. He lives up in the attic, and we only visit him secretly, in hushed tones. But the point of the Christian gospel is that in Jesus Christ the true God invited himself to dinner and became quite literally the life and soul of the party – and now invites us to feast with him and to discover, by getting to know him, what a genuinely human existence, a life flooded with God's love and energy and wisdom, might start to look like, in public as well as in private. That feast itself, the feast to which Jesus now invites us, speaks of a strange flourishing, a dying and rising again, a losing all to find all, a call to follow him to the cross, to lead by serving, to discover the meaning of the Beatitudes which speak of the poor, the meek and the persecuted inheriting not just heaven but also the earth. This vision is so out of tune with contemporary Western attitudes that it is bound to sound strange and awkward when voiced in public. But we must do so none the less.

This is the strange public truth of the Christian gospel. God is in the business of remaking the whole world, turning it the right way up at last. The call of the Christian gospel makes the sense it's supposed to make, not when it is heard as a call to ignore the world and pursue a private salvation, but when it is heard as a call to follow Jesus and become part of his plan to sort the world out now, as much as we can, in advance of the final day. Being a Christian means that your own life becomes part of that anticipation, allowing God to do in your heart and mind, your imagination and energy, what he's going to do one day for the whole world – that is, remake it from top to bottom and flood it with his glory. When that starts to happen, it can never, in the nature of the case, be something that happens to you all by yourself. It is bound to constitute a call that you, in turn, will become part of the solution, obedient to whatever God calls you to do as part of his plan for the wider world. At that point, you become part of the meaning of 'God in public'.

In pondering that vocation, we glance for one last time at the larger global scene. Tomorrow's world is, to be sure, a place of great danger, great uncertainty and great opportunity. That world urgently needs energetic people who will allow their lives to be transformed and transforming. We've tried all the other ways, the ways that keep God out of the picture. Let us not be put off by the squeals of the secularists on the one hand or the follies of the fundamentalists on the other. We need people to be part of the story of God in public, to live and speak and act truly, wisely and fruitfully for him in tomorrow's world.

7

God's powerful foolishness in a world of foolish power

I have a hunch that some at least of our problems in today's Western world stem from the fact that we have forgotten how the biblical theme of power actually works. We have run up against all sorts of questions to do with power, but we have not found it natural or easy to turn for help to the profound things the New Testament has to say. As a result, we have simply maintained the traditions of power which were and are well known in the world, and we have failed to grapple with the genuinely Christian alternative.

Indeed, one might not know that there *was* a Christian alternative. But it is clear, right across the pages of the New Testament. And perhaps nowhere more so than in the passage from which the chapter title, as you may have realized, is taken. Paul, getting into his stride as he confronts the arrogant and faction-ridden Corinthians, says it in a wonderful rhetorical flourish, all the more powerful for being ironic in a passage where he's saying that rhetoric isn't what matters:

> The word of the cross, you see, is madness to people who are being destroyed. But to us – those who are being saved – it is God's power . . . In God's wisdom, the world didn't know God through wisdom, so it gave God pleasure, through the folly of our proclamation, to save those who believe. Jews look for signs, you see, and Greeks search for wisdom; but we announce the crucified Messiah, a scandal to Jews and folly to Gentiles, but to those who are called, Jews and Greeks alike, the Messiah – God's power and God's wisdom.

Then here it is, the line from which my chapter title is taken: 'For God's folly is wiser than humans, you see, and God's weakness is stronger than humans' (1 Corinthians 1.18–25).

And Paul then goes on to explain in more detail what he means. Starting with this passage, I shall explain a little about what Paul meant in the context of his letter to Corinth. That will open things up for me to say something about where this teaching might relate to us today. That in turn will demand that we turn to other biblical passages in the quest for a rounded view of God's foolish power, or rather, we might say, the foolish weakness of God which turns out to contain the power of wisdom.

Folly and wisdom, weakness and power: the gospel in Corinth

Corinth in Paul's day was a Roman colony. Like most colonies then and now it took a special pride in modelling itself, as far as possible, on the mother city. Among the many challenges facing Christians in Corinth was the question of how much of the local culture one could and should go along with, and how much had to be resisted in the name of Jesus and according to the logic of the gospel. We can watch Paul working this out at various points of the letter, as he tackles issues about lawsuits, about sex and marriage, about food offered to idols, and so on. Anyone who has studied 1 Corinthians even at a basic level will be well aware of these things.

But among the other challenges of living as a follower of Jesus in a world where the wisdom of Greece had been merged in with the culture of Rome was the question of social hierarchy and prestige. Roman society had been organized on hierarchical lines for many generations. Not only were there two big lines down the middle, the first between the free and the slaves and the second between men and women. At the top of the tree you would find the senatorial class, with a clear line between them and the powerful upper-middle class called the 'knights', and then another clear line before you got to the lower orders, who were further subdivided. Enormous weight was put on family breeding and connections, on the one hand, and on wealth and property, on the other. There was always the possibility that people might be able to move up the social ladder, but they had to be very talented and very bright – and extremely hard-working and probably very lucky too – if they were going to do so. The obvious example of someone with all of that was Cicero.

But then, in the century between Cicero and Paul, an even greater hierarchy was born. The old Roman republic was in tatters, and the new empire emerged from its ruins. The emperor himself, supreme over all, was hailed as 'son of god'. Where you have an emperor, you have a court; and where you have a court you have a new kind of social ranking within and alongside the older ones. In a colony like Corinth, eager to demonstrate its ability to be more Roman than Rome itself, everybody would know exactly where they stood in the local pecking order.

To be sure, this is not the only problem which Paul is addressing in the first two chapters of the letter, but I think it is near the heart. As he says, not many of the Corinthian Christians were part of the upper levels of the social hierarchy. Not many were noble born or powerful in human terms (1.26). They didn't have much clout, or cut much ice, in the wider society. But it seems, from things Paul says later on, that the Christians were grasping on to their newfound faith in Jesus as the true son of God, the true lord of the world, as a social lever, a way of pulling themselves up in the world. And when people do that they start to organize themselves unofficially into parties and groups, clinging often enough to the coat-tails of this or that teacher. 'I belong to Paul', 'I belong to Apollos', 'I belong to Cephas', and then the mysterious fourth group, 'I belong to Christ' (1.12). And with all this, Paul declares, they are simply playing the world's games: the world's games of apparent *wisdom*, playing off this teacher against that; the world's games of apparent *power*, seeking to gain status and prestige in a world where that mattered above almost everything else.

I suspect that many Christians today, though they might recognize that the Corinthians were going about things in the wrong way, wouldn't regard it as all that much of a problem in comparison with some of the things Paul mentions later in the letter. Scholars sometimes talk about the 'honour–shame' culture in the world of Paul's day, sometimes going so far as to suggest that this is strange to us because we have no contemporary equivalent. But this is actually ridiculous. We have just as much an honour–shame culture as they did. The way we dress, the kind of car we drive, the letters we have after our names, the way we educate our children, and so on and so on – the Western world is just as much organized around status and pride as Paul's world was, though the signals and symbols of our honour and shame are undeniably different. And we have, rather obviously, a far more divided church than anything Paul could have imagined. Paul knew of four divisions in the church; most of us could list a lot more than that within twenty miles of our homes. And the divisions between our churches today, just as we may suspect they were in Paul's day, can be mapped in some ways on to the lines we draw across our world. The church, right from the start, has tended to take its cue from the society around it, and to use aspects of the Christian faith, particularly specific doctrines or practices, as weapons in the ongoing implicit social and cultural contest.

This is obviously so in British society, and has been for a long time. In the eighteenth century, the Anglicans were often the middle or upper-middle classes, with the working classes embracing the new Methodist movement. Even within Methodism, there were social divisions: in the small town where I grew up there were two Methodist churches, whose main difference apparently was that the servants went to the one and the masters to the other. (All that has now changed.) Meanwhile, the Roman Catholic churches in many parts of mainland Britain were largely full of Irish immigrants, who tended to be from the labouring classes, and a small number of older Recusant families proud of their Catholic connections going back to the sixteenth century. And so on. As I look across the Atlantic at North American society today I see similar things etched rather obviously into its church life, where the combination of the 'culture wars' with the present political polarizations – that's already quite a toxic mixture right there – is played out in terms of different theologies, ecclesial styles and ethical stances. And I think Paul would have a sharp word or two to say about all this.

But my point is not just about the unity of the church, vital and thoroughly Pauline though that is. It has deeper political and spiritual roots, and noticing that will take us towards the main thing I want to say. As Paul's argument in 1 Corinthians continues into (what we call) chapter 2, he agrees that the gospel does generate its own kind of wisdom, but he differentiates this sharply from what he calls 'the wisdom of this age or the rulers of this age'. He is offering through the gospel, he says, a different kind of wisdom which had been secret and hidden. It was, he says, prepared by God from long ago 'for our glory'. But this wisdom, he goes on, had remained hidden from the power-brokers of the world: 'None of the rulers of this present age knew about this wisdom. If they had, you see, they wouldn't have crucified the Lord of glory' (1 Corinthians 2.8). That is a fascinating remark, sweeping aside at a stroke the power structures of Paul's day or of any day. Who was it who crucified Jesus? It was that other deadly combination, the Judaean leadership on the one hand, defending their position at the top of the Temple-based hierarchy, and Caesar's empire on the other, defending itself as it always did against any threat of rebel leadership. But what is Paul saying about them, about these people who seemed to be at the top of the tree when it came to power? He is saying three things which resonate out into our own world of foolish power.

First, he is saying that the ultimate wisdom through which God wants to run the world is a different kind of wisdom from anything the world's power-brokers understand. It is, as he goes on to say, a wisdom which is revealed through the Spirit, a wisdom which builds up the church as a single organism, the single Temple of the living God; and the rulers of this world didn't even glimpse it. They had no idea there was any way to create human community except their own way, the way of foolish power, the way that crushes and crucifies all opposition.

Second, he is therefore saying that God has revealed in Jesus the Messiah, and goes on revealing through the Spirit to Jesus' followers, the real kind of wisdom which the rulers didn't know; *and that this wisdom is the source of the Christian's actual glory.* Jesus is the 'Lord of glory', the one who is now already enthroned as the true world ruler. And his followers, those who belong to him, who are 'in him', members of his body, are intended by God to be 'glorified' with him. This doesn't mean that they will one day share in the radiance of his light in God's new world, though Paul may perhaps be envisaging that as well. It means that they are already – that we are already – charged, tasked, with the vocation to be glory-bearers in the world. We are indeed to be the people through whom God is ruling his world, but not in the way the power-brokers do it. Here is Paul's challenge. The Corinthians are within touching distance of exercising the real authority which, delegated from Jesus himself, will make them world-transformers. But they are swapping that for their own small versions of the kind of power which is normal in the world, the foolish power which only knows how to crucify people. Instead, throughout this letter, and even more in the second letter he writes to the same church in Corinth, Paul is telling them to lift up their eyes and glimpse the power and glory which are in fact supposed to be theirs. It is a totally different kind of power and glory. This is a message for our time just as much as for his.

What is this power and glory? Here is the third thing he is saying, in a typically dense phrase which might just run right by us if we didn't stop and ponder it: 'None of the rulers of this age knew about this wisdom,' he writes. 'If they had, you see, they wouldn't have crucified the Lord of glory.' Why not? What would have stopped them? Answer: the cross itself contains, expresses, embodies and unveils the power that made the earth and sea and sky, the glory that rules the world and everything in it. *By crucifying Jesus, the rulers of this age did the very thing which enabled Jesus to win the decisive victory over them, because his crucifixion was the ultimate expression of God's love, which was and is the power which conquers and rules the world.* It was the power of utter self-giving love, the power by which the creator right from the start said 'Let it be', bringing into existence in sheer generosity a world that was and is other than himself.

The early Christian Fathers sometimes expounded this verse in terms of God setting a trap for the worldly authorities, and even for the diabolical powers that lurk in the shadows behind them. These powers all work according to the foolish power of the world: the diabolical forces are basically anti-creation forces, determined to ruin God's wonderful created order and to prevent its rescue and renewal. That is why they operate, among other ways, through the foolish worldly power which exercises its hollow authority by destroying and killing, whereas God the glorious creator exercises his majestic authority by the powerful foolishness which is unveiled in the gospel, by pouring out his own lifeblood to rescue, redeem and restore. That is why the aim and goal of the gospel, as Paul says again and again, is new creation: not the destruction of the present world, with a few people escaping from it to go off elsewhere, but the redemption of creation, and of humans as its first-fruits. Such humans are then to become in their turn the agents of the foolish but ultimately victorious power of love let loose in the world. Right here, in the opening salvo of one of his greatest letters, Paul declares that the foolishness of God is wiser than the human world, and the weakness of God is stronger than the human world. He thus confronts the Corinthians, as they get lured into playing out the world's power-games even on the little stage of the church itself, with the challenge to a different way, a more excellent way, the way of love.

Now it would be fun to chase this through 1 Corinthians itself, and we could easily spend the entire chapter doing that. But I want just to back up what I've been saying with one quick glance at the letter to the Colossians, and then move to consider in more detail the ways in which our world, and sadly our church, needs to hear this message today. This will send us back to the gospels themselves to see the way in which this same contrast of two types of power is woven into their structure and central message.

In the second chapter of Colossians, Paul again describes the cross as a strange, paradoxical victory over the powers of the world. He is in the process of describing how the ancient Jewish law, with its codes and specific restrictions, no longer applies to those who belong to the Messiah. They are already complete in him; they already have his wisdom as their own, his divine life as the very place where they are to dwell. They have been brought from death to life through his death and life, leaving behind in his tomb all the sin and wickedness which had threatened to kill them for ever. Then he says that God erased, rubbed out, 'the handwriting that was against us, opposing us with its legal demands. He took it right out of the way, by nailing it to the cross.' That is a message most Christians probably understand fairly well. But Paul then sets it in the wider context of the larger victory which God was winning on Calvary: 'He stripped the rulers and authorities of their armour, and displayed them contemptuously to public view, celebrating his triumph over them in him' (Colossians 2.15).

Paul knows perfectly well how extraordinary and paradoxical this was. The crucifixion looked for all the world, and *to* all the world, as though the rulers and authorities were disarming *Jesus*, making a public example of *him*, celebrating a triumph over him. But in fact, he says, it was the other way round. When you learn to see the cross as God sees the cross, you see it inside out. The cross was where the world *did* all that it could, and God *gave* all that he *was*. The cross was where the world defended its own power by doing what it did best, killing and crushing all opposition; and it was where God revealed his own power by doing what he has done from the very beginning, loving the world and giving it new life. The cross was where the powerful foolishness of God defeated the foolish power of the world. That larger, cosmic narrative frames, and makes sense of, all the more sharply focused things that Paul says about power and the cross.

I tear myself away from the contemplation of the cross itself in order to ask: where does the shoe pinch for us? Where does the foolish power of today's world stand in shame before the revelation of God's powerful foolishness in the gospel?

Power and folly in today's world

Let me first remind you of three places – there are many more, but these are well known – where God's powerful foolishness has in fact been seen at work in our world. When I was in my twenties, the world looked on as South Africa threatened to collapse in a bloodbath, an orgy of interracial war. Many commentators took it for granted that a major civil war was on the way, and that we would just have to sit back and watch. There was a kind of Social Darwinian shoulder-shrugging mood about it: the thing would have to play itself out. But God had raised up a man who spent three or four hours every morning in prayer and the rest of the day in faithful and risky witness to a different way, the way of reconciliation. If you had said in 1975 that a young black priest, then newly appointed Dean of the Cathedral in Johannesburg, would within twenty years be chairing, as Archbishop, a Commission for Truth and Reconciliation at which white thugs and black thugs would come and confess their appalling crimes and seek personal and national reconciliation, the world would have laughed in your face. But it happened. Civil war was averted. There are of course still enormous problems facing South Africa. Tutu has continued to address those, earning himself unpopularity with the present rulers as he did for different reasons with their predecessors. But the problems can now be faced in a new light. God's powerful foolishness triumphed over the foolish power both of the apartheid regime and of those bent on revolutionary violence.

Then, as we know, there was the fall of communism. Again, when I was young it looked as though Eastern Europe was going to stay communist for ever. The Cold War was in full swing. Some even hailed it as the balance of power that was preventing a third world war, and a nuclear one at that. But God had raised up a man of prayer to be a bishop, then an archbishop, in Poland, and to everyone's astonishment he was elected Pope just when his own country was about to launch the initial protest, the 'Solidarity' movement, that brought down Polish communism and revealed that the other regimes all around were likewise brittle and fragile, for all their massive and clunky apparatus of foolish power. It still brings tears to my eyes as I remember the crowds in Wenceslas Square in Prague in what was then Czechoslovakia, those evenings in 1989, standing with candles in prayerful protest. They didn't have tanks and guns. The way to defeat the foolish power of the world is not by imitating it, by taking it on with its own methods. The way to defeat it is with the powerful foolishness of God. Prague is not Poland. It lacks any deep-rooted popular Catholicism or any other form of Christianity. But those people were praying that night, invoking a different sort of power; and their prayers were answered. Undoubtedly, Eastern Europe still faces enormous problems. But they can be faced in a new light.

The third example isn't another archbishop. Or even – in a world where leadership was still normally male – a man. When I was young, people who were approaching death, especially from unpleasant illnesses, were either looked after in ordinary (and often inadequate) hospital wards, or sent home to die there. The doctors basically gave them up. To many in the medical profession, a dying patient represented failure. It wasn't worth spending more time and money on them. Many therefore died in sad, and sometimes squalid, conditions. But God was raising up a woman of faith and courage, a woman who had seen people she loved dying under these conditions, and who knew in her bones that the love of God should be reflected in a completely different approach. And Cicely Saunders founded the first of the modern hospices in London, without help from the government, in the teeth of opposition from the medical profession, raising the money herself. She sent a signal of hope, just at the moment when people in the UK and USA were starting to talk, as secularists do, of euthanasia or assisted suicide. The movement has spread rapidly around Britain and the world. I am proud that the UK is now a world leader in palliative care, which models the powerful foolishness of God, sending that sign of hope into millions of families who have learned to face death with dignity and trust. Undeniably, death is still a vicious and horrible enemy. But it can be faced in a new light.

I mention these three very different instances of the powerful foolishness of God overcoming the foolish power of the world in order to highlight the fact that in so many other areas of our national and international life we simply haven't got to first base.

When push comes to shove we still reach for violence as the basic solution to all problems. We still play the game of foolish power in one arena after another. We allowed our financial systems to bring half the world into massive and unpayable debt, which we refused to write off, talking grandly about people needing to learn the rules of the game. Then when our own banks and businesses suddenly failed because they got too greedy and careless, we wrote off their debts in a flash because we couldn't imagine a world where the power of mammon was not one of the foundation-stones. As I said in an earlier chapter, the very rich did for the very rich what they had refused to do, and still refuse to do, for the very poor. Our honour–shame culture insists that the rich and powerful must be enabled to stay rich and powerful. But if we were to adjust our standards of honour and shame according to the foolish power of God in the gospel, then the needs of the poor, at home and abroad, would always be at the top of the agenda.

Obviously this isn't easy. There are always complicating factors. I'm not talking about collapsing into some new form of socialism or communism where people simply become dependent on an increasingly inflated government machine, allowing corruption and inefficiency to run riot. But our systems have gone on far too long using that danger as a scare tactic to make us all think that the only way to go is to keep using the system of riches and power we know, love and secretly worship, even if we privately recognize that it is both inefficient in itself and desperately divisive socially. And, God help us, our churches frequently join in the game, using the money which we have in abundance in the West to bribe poorer churches elsewhere in the world to collude with our own agendas in the squabbles within our international denominations. There must be a different way, a way which would embody the Magnificat, Mary's song, a way which would embody the powerful foolishness of God.

And then of course there is the military adventurism that has defaced recent years. Here too things are inevitably complicated, but there are certain points which should stand out. American troops eventually killed Osama bin Laden (an extra-legal act which itself raised questions for many), but his horrible and wicked act on September 11, 2001 has had exactly the effect he hoped it would. It has lured the Western nations, especially the UK and USA, into long and bitter struggles in Iraq and Afghanistan, providing exactly the reinforcement for the Islamist myth of Western violence and tyranny which bin Laden knew perfectly well would recruit thousands more to his cause. Every bomb we have dropped in that region has had that effect, as one could easily see in advance.

On the day I am preparing this chapter for publication (14 November 2015) over 120 people have been killed in a coordinated terrorist attack in Paris. In response to all these things, we have killed not only terrorists (and terrorists are simply human beings who are driven to do terrible things because they, or the people who hood-wink them or compel them, see no alternative), but also hundreds of thousands of innocent bystanders, making them curse not only us but also what they take to be our religion. We have, astonishingly, allowed troops to do unspeakable things and claim to be acting as Christians, once more solidifying the belief of many in the Middle East that Christianity is a crusading religion that wants to conquer the world by the foolish power of guns and bombs and death. And all the while our closest continuing allies in the Middle East include some countries which are hugely oppressive, where you might be in serious trouble for even owning a Bible, and would certainly be in deep trouble if you tried to celebrate Holy Communion in your home or a hotel room. We have operated double, triple and quadruple standards, often driven by money – think of the contracts to rebuild bits of Iraq that were signed, to the great advantage of some in Western governments, before the first bombs were even dropped! – and always with the bottom line that we have firmly believed that the way to solve problems in the world is through military might.

After the First World War, when many in Germany were near starvation, Winston Churchill proposed sending ships loaded with food and medical supplies, as an act of magnanimity and generosity, and in the desire to rebuild a better Europe. The British Parliament refused the proposal. Who can tell how the 1920s and 1930s would have turned out had they agreed? In the same way, supposing we used the money and high technology we are currently employing on drone warfare – itself a strange innovation with all kinds of dark resonances – to send help to the millions in the Middle East who are neither tyrants nor terrorists but our fellow human beings facing appalling conditions? Would that not send a very different message?

Might it not actually slow down the drive to recruit more young people to fight the 'great satan' they see in the West?

I hope this will not be misunderstood. I am not a pacifist (to the disappointment of some of my friends). I do believe that there are times, and I think the Second World War at least was one of those times, when armed resistance to tyranny and invasion may be justified. Just as the police are justified in using force, and if necessary violence, to restrain and restrict people who are themselves bent on violence and wickedness, and to protect the vulnerable and innocent, so such times may arise on the global stage. But a police force only really works if it is seen and believed to be basically neutral, on the side of stability and justice in society, and in particular on the side of the poor and needy, rather than working for one side in a social or cultural divide. And any suggestion that the USA and UK, with a few friends here and there, could ever be in that position in international affairs would be simply laughable. We need to see ourselves as others see us, and to realize that much of the world regards us as the big bullies, the over-muscled thugs who use the foolish power that has always been typical of empires. So many of our actions seem to reinforce this message, and we need to understand why some have concluded that their only possible response is terrorism.

Once more, please do not misunderstand. I am not saying there are not dangerous things going on in the world, or that the terrorists are not wicked, or that we do not have a responsibility to play our part in making the world a safer place. I am making two points. First, the pragmatic one. Our efforts in that direction over the last decade or two have actually made the world a much *less* safe place, so that even if we changed course this minute we would still leave for our children and grandchildren a legacy of bitterness and resentment across many countries and peoples who have seen their lives ruined by a bomb or a drone or by the unleashing of fresh sectarian and tribal violence in the wake of our blunderings. Second, the theological one. What we have done has nothing of the finger-prints of the gospel about it. Nothing. We have colluded with the split-level world of the Enlightenment, which has decreed that religion is about what happens in the heavenly world, where we enjoy a private spirituality and a future disembodied hope, leaving the world to do its own thing, again by the means of Social Darwinism. We have assumed that the only way to get things done is by the foolish power of the world.

There are, undeniably, a fair number of pacifist protesters in the West, and there is the noble Anabaptist tradition that has represented a radically different way. But I have yet to see anyone articulating the equivalent, in today's dangerous world, of what Desmond Tutu was doing in South Africa. Tutu's way was all about prayer, and then it was all about dangerous and Bible-based confrontation and negotiation, both with the white government who saw him as a grinning monkey and with the black activists who called him an Uncle Tom for rejecting their way of violence. Where is the new generation of Christian leaders in our world who will run the same risks out of prayerful love for the Jesus who embodied the powerful foolishness of the love of God?

I raise these questions not knowing the answer, but knowing that it is long past time to be looking for it. Our problem runs very, very deep. As children of the Enlightenment (to say it yet again), we have said to ourselves for two hundred years that we are the elite, the grown-up ones, the leading edge of world civilization. We have built up a myth about our own place and role in the world, so that we have really come to believe that it is our divine right to run things, to call the shots, to rescue the world from any mess it might get in, to punish wicked people on our own terms. To go back for a moment to the 'drone strikes': there is an alarming parallel between that kind of event and the picture that many Western Christians have of a God who sits up in the sky and occasionally 'zaps' this or that person or place. We should perhaps ponder the ways in which our practice, even in supposedly 'non-religious' areas of life, reflects some of our unthought-out theology. Anyway, we in the West now sometimes worry whether our assumed world dominance might now be forfeited to another country, to China for instance or perhaps India – not just because it could be very inconvenient but because it would completely undermine the modernist narrative on which we have lived for so long. But, again, the idea of one country or another leading the world and telling it what to do – which Britain was very good at doing for a hundred years, which I fear may be where America got the idea from in the first place! – is itself simply another manifestation of the foolish power of the world.

Take another example. When we look at ancient maps of the world we smile indulgently at the way in which in some such designs Jerusalem was placed at the centre, with everything else radiating out from there. But we have our own versions. Modern Western European cartographers have regularly drawn maps of the world in which Western Europe just happened to sit aesthetically in the golden section, even though that has regularly meant seeing many parts of the world as much smaller and less significant than they actually are. In these and many other ways we have imposed our own self-serving myths on several areas of culture and global life. This cannot last. As a matter of history, modern Western civilization will sooner or later go the way of Greece and Rome, not least because it has undermined itself by its own internal corruptions. Our modern Western culture owes a great deal to Christianity; we thank God, for instance, for the wonderful art and music which came from Europe's deep Christian roots and is still cherished by millions even if they do not share the faith which originally produced it. But we must not be fooled into thinking that therefore we can rest content with our present mode of culture, or that we can hail it as automatically 'Judaeo-Christian' in an uncritical fashion. We must be alive and alert to the fact that the only power which matters is the powerful foolishness of God, revealed in the cross of Jesus the Messiah, rather than the foolish power of the world.

These are just some of the ways in which it seems to me that Western culture has embraced the agendas and methods which in the New Testament are seen as precisely the way 'the rulers of the world' have always gone about things. And the tragedy is that we in the churches have routinely assumed the myth of Western supremacy, or even the myth of American manifest destiny and/or exceptionalism (and, before that, the British equivalent!), so that we have simply failed to apply the biblical critique of ordinary foolish power to ourselves and our institutions. I want now to look back to the New Testament, and this time to the gospels, to see yet more clearly why this ought to be regarded as an urgent task.

Jesus and power: the different way

There are many places in the gospels where we might begin to examine the question of God's foolish power. The Jesus who at the end of Matthew's gospel declares that all authority has been given to him – a statement of universal sovereignty rooted in the ancient vision of the Messiah's role in the Psalms and the Prophets – is the Jesus who was born with threats from the world's rulers, in his case Herod, following him into an enforced exile. Matthew rubs in the point: Jesus' name is Emmanuel, God With Us (Matthew 1.23). When the living and all-powerful God comes to live in our midst, what it looks like is a tiny refugee, a newborn baby with a price on his head. Then there is the striking scene in Luke when Jesus and the disciples come to a village which refuses to receive them, and James and John, aptly named the 'sons of thunder', want to do what Elijah had done in the Old Testament, namely to call down fire from heaven and burn them all up. That, of course, is precisely what we still like to do with people who oppose us: our technology can produce fine-tuned 'fire from heaven' to order. But Jesus rebukes them (Luke 9.51–56). That is not the way.

What Jesus then does, which comes out perhaps clearest in Luke's gospel, is to take upon himself the judgment which might have fallen on God's rebel people. He goes to his death as the green stick when it was the dry ones that were ready for burning (Luke 23.28–31). And, when he comes to Jerusalem, Luke makes it clear that this is what it looks like when Israel's God returns at last to his people as he had always promised to do. He comes not in a blazing fire, not in a pillar of cloud and fire, not on the chariot with whirling wheels such as Ezekiel saw, but as a young prophet in tears, riding into the city on a donkey (Luke 19.28–41).

No wonder people over the last two centuries (to look no further) poured scorn on Christianity, a movement which came to something of a climax when Friedrich Nietzsche referred to the Christian vision as a slave mentality. It offered, he said, a weak and pathetic view of the world, encouraging people to be feeble and helpless rather than embodying what he called the 'will to power' which alone would master the universe. Well, Nietzsche's vision was implemented by the Nazis, as far as they could, and look where that got us. But the trouble is that, though we all shudder at the mention of Nazi Germany, we have built up our own version of Nietzsche's Superman-myth, of the will to power which will sweep away all weakness and human inadequacy before our own all-conquering worldview with its high-energy military power. And we – we, including devout Christians! – have carved up the four gospels so that they *only* speak about Jesus as the divine son of God whose death will enable us to go to heaven, instead of reading their full message, which is about the living God becoming king on earth as in heaven. This happens in and through Jesus; yes, in his healing and celebration and mighty deeds, but also, supremely and decisively, in his death on the cross.

This comes to a head in Mark's gospel when, once again, James and John get the wrong end of the stick, eager as always to use the world's foolish power rather than the powerful foolishness which Jesus had already been articulating in telling them to take up the cross and follow him. They come to him and request, in a passage we looked at in a previous chapter (Mark 10.35–45), that they will be allowed to sit at his right and left when he arrives in his glory, that is, in his kingly power. Like the Corinthians, they have in mind the ordinary worldly rankings in which people can have their egos boosted, their names on everybody's lips, their status assured. Perhaps James would be Jesus' Chief of Staff, and John would be his Secretary for Homeland Policy, or whatever. His right and his left hands. Perhaps they already dreamed of the kind of lifestyle that they might then enjoy . . . the kind of thing that the Herods and the Caesars of this world enjoy, the fruits of their foolish power.

Jesus explains to them that this is not the way. He provides perhaps the clearest statement of the contrasting types of power we find anywhere in scripture (though actually the theme goes back once more to the Psalms and the Prophets, particularly to Isaiah where the little child leads the formerly violent animals into a paradise of peace, and where the Servant of the Lord is the one because of whom the kings of the earth will shut their mouths). Note how, at the end of this paragraph, Jesus' statement of intent in terms of his own death emphasizes, just as Paul does in 1 Corinthians, the reversal of power. It is not about leaving the world behind and escaping to heaven. It is about the new way in which the world is to be transformed:

> Jesus called them to him. 'You know how it is in the pagan nations,' he said. 'Think how their so-called rulers act. They lord it over their subjects. The high and mighty ones boss the rest around. But that's not how it's going to be with you. Anyone who wants to be great among you must become your servant. Anyone who wants to be first must be

everyone's slave. Don't you see? The son of man didn't come to be waited on. He came to be the servant, to give his life "as a ransom for many".'   (Mark 10.42–45)

This is a marvellous, vital passage. As with 1 Corinthians, or with John (where we shall go in a moment), we could spend a chapter on it alone. But I hope the basic points stand out.

First, Jesus is acknowledging that the world has its own way of power, of the foolish power which comes from lording it over people, tyrannizing them, bossing and bullying, backing it all up with force, and if necessary with death itself. Notice that Jesus does not say, as we in the West might have expected him to say, 'But how the world exercises power is irrelevant for us, because we are not going to stick around in this world; we are on the way to heaven, and we'll leave Caesar and his folks to do what they like.' That has been a standard Western view for a long time now, but it is clearly not what Jesus is saying.

Second, Jesus is presupposing, as he does throughout his public career, that God is launching his kingdom on earth as in heaven, which makes it rather urgent to ask the question, what sort of a kingdom will this be? Here it is clear that the kingdom will be put into effect, not by the love of power but by the power of love, not by the foolish power of the tyrants of the world but by the powerful foolishness of the Servant.

Third, Jesus is combining Daniel 7, with the exaltation of the son of man, with Isaiah 53, the servant who came to give his life as a ransom for many. He is claiming thereby that in his death he will not only exemplify and model what this servant-ministry looks like, but will actually – somehow! – accomplish the take-over of power from the bullies and the tyrants. When the son of man is exalted to the right hand of God after his suffering at the hands of the monsters, as in Daniel 7, he will indeed be the world's true lord, and his followers will indeed be doing his work and bringing the world into conformity with his rule. But that rule will be established in the first place, and implemented thereafter, not by the foolish power of the tyrant but by the powerful foolishness of the crucified Messiah.

There are many other passages to which we might turn as we reflect on this theme. We could go to the book of Revelation, where the violent imagery is not intended (as people have often wrongly imagined it) as a metonym for actual violence. The violent language is metaphorical and symbolic, expressing the victory of the slaughtered Lamb. Or we could look at 1 Peter, where the church is puzzled at its own harsh suffering – if we are the followers of Jesus, why should all this be happening to us? – and they are assured that this is indeed the way in which the kingdom of Jesus is making its way in the world. But I want to end with John's gospel, and with a passage which has a good claim to be the centre of all Christian political theology: chapters 18 and 19, where Jesus stands before Pontius Pilate, the kingdom of God confronting the kingdom of Caesar, the power of love calling time on the love of power. The confrontation, and its result, embodies exactly the same sequence we have seen in Paul and in Mark, only this time highlighted in terms of an actual conversation (see also chapter 3 above).

It begins in John 18.33 with Pilate asking Jesus whether he is in fact king of the Jews. After an initial clarification, Jesus does indeed claim a kingdom, but he declares that it isn't the usual sort; it is not the sort that grows in this world. Jesus rams home the point: if my kingdom was the sort that grows in this world, he explains, *my followers would be fighting* to prevent me from being handed over. Exactly as in Mark, this is explicitly a different sort of kingdom from those of the bullies and tyrants.

How then does the kingdom make its way? Jesus appears to change the subject, but in fact he goes to the heart of it. 'I have come', he says, 'to bear witness to the truth.' Pilate, famously, answers 'What is truth?' We have come to think of that as the sneer of the postmodernist, the cynic; but it is equally the sneer of the high-pressure imperialist: we are in power here, we make our own truth, we decide what's going to be true in the world and we enforce it by any means necessary. But throughout John's gospel Jesus has been speaking and modelling a different sort of truth. Truth, for Jesus, is what happens when human beings, in obedience to God the creator, speak words which bring God's fresh order into the world. Truth is an *event*, a creative, restorative, healing, judging, reordering phenomenon. And Jesus not only speaks the truth, bringing that fresh new-creation order to the world. He *is* the truth, the living word which the creator God has spoken both to bring the judging and healing truth into the old world and to bring about the new world that is waiting to be born on Easter morning.

This then moves into the discussion of power. Pilate has power over Jesus, so he claims; the power to have him killed, or to release him. Jesus agrees; Pilate really does have that power, and, astonishingly to us, that power has been given him by God himself. The point, as we have noticed at various stages throughout this book, is that God wants human authorities to run his world, but he will hold them to account for how they do it. But meanwhile Jesus is the one with real power – and Pilate, exactly as in 1 Corinthians, sends Jesus to his death, and thereby destroys the foundation of his own shaky imperial power. Jesus' death, in John as in Mark, as in Revelation, as in Paul, is the victory by which the foolish power of the world is overcome by the powerful foolishness of God.

So how do the 'traditional' meanings of the cross make sense within this larger narrative? The answer is that they make all the sense in the world. The point about Jesus dying for my sins, for our sins – which is such a powerful and personal truth that it ought to sweep us off our feet again and again, however many times we have heard it – is that the kingdom of God which is established through Jesus' death goes, as it were, right through the system from top to bottom. It defeats the power of violence by dying with a prayer on its lips, defusing the anger and the spirals of recrimination that would otherwise be perpetuated. But it defeats thereby also the power of sin which has had us in its grip, taking its shame and its grim entail of death and exhausting that as well. The powers of the world rule the world because we humans have abdicated our own power as God's image-bearers; our sin has rendered us impotent. But if our sins have been dealt with, then this transfer of power to the dark forces that have taken over the world is nullified. This is why, in Galatians 1.4, Paul declares that the Messiah 'gave himself for our sins to rescue us from the present evil age'. The powers get their power from our sin, but our sin was dealt with on the cross. In his death, as Isaiah saw, the Messiah took the punishment which was due, the exile and death which are inscribed across the story of Israel as they are across the story of the world, and drew them to a single place where they were dealt with once and for all and for ever.

The integration of those multiple meanings of the cross is why we are not just forgiven our sins, but set free so that we can now be part of Jesus' kingdom-project, bringing his alternative kingdom, by its alternative means, to bear on the life of the whole world. That is more or less exactly what John the Divine saw in Revelation 5.9–10: the slaughtered Lamb has 'purchased a people for God . . . and made them a kingdom and priests to our God, and they will reign on the earth'.

Conclusion

There is much that we could go on to discuss at this point. There are many potential spin-offs from this in both personal and public life. True, some might want to say that we simply have to make a split, with Christians following Jesus' alternative way in their private lives but with countries and governments continuing the normal way of the world. You will realize that I believe that would be dangerous folly, however much it is *de facto* what the Western world has done, and what the Western church has colluded with, for many years. I know only too well that the attempts at a kind of Christian 'theocracy' that have been tried from time to time have not been a great success (to put it mildly), and that one might well use that fact as a warning against even starting down that road. But I cannot, as a reader of the New Testament, shake the strong conviction that when Jesus taught us to pray that God's kingdom would come and his will be done on earth as in heaven, and when he went about doing the kingdom and then dying to make it happen at last, this was not a kingdom to be glimpsed by consenting adults in private, but a kingdom which was designed to confront, as it did then confront, the bullies and the tyrants of the world with the news, with the *fact*, that there is a different way of doing power. I believe the Western world, with its unrivalled technological and similar skills, and with its recent history of failed and damaging attempts once more to do the worldly thing of foolish power, is overdue for a look at the radical alternative.

It won't be popular, just as James and John no doubt were horribly disappointed by Jesus' answer. It will certainly lead to misunderstanding. It may very well lead to suffering. But if we are following Jesus there should be no alternative. He, as Paul says, has been made unto us wisdom, righteousness, sanctification and redemption. He is the one whose cross unveils the secret of how the world really works, the secret kept hidden from the beginning, the secret the rulers of the world never knew. In him and his death we see at last the foolishness of God which is wiser than all human wisdom, the weakness of God which is stronger than all human strength. If as Christians we claim the name, presence and power of Jesus the Messiah in our lives; if we claim the Bible as our key to God's revelation and the cross as the centre of our faith; if as human beings we are fed up with the abuses of power in our world – then we cannot ignore what the Bible itself says so clearly about the cross and its meaning. It is time to take Paul more seriously, to take Mark and John more seriously, to take Jesus himself more seriously. It is time to put aside the foolish power of the world and to embrace, whatever it may cost, the powerful foolishness of God.

8

Christian virtue in peace and war

My topic here is a difficult one, and as always when in difficulties one must stress character. The point about character, and within that virtue, is grasped when we see where these words come from. 'Character' comes from the Greek for 'stamp', as in the mark which is stamped on wax, metal or paper. 'Virtue' comes from the Latin for 'strength', and indicates the strengths of character which are developed into patterns of thought, action and even feeling. The point is that when these virtues are made firm within us, they come to be stamped so deep that they show up in our behaviour whether we're thinking hard about it or not – in fact, particularly when we aren't. I want to begin this chapter, then, by going briefly through what we mean by 'virtue', following that up by addressing some of the regular problems that people have seen with the notion. I then want to look at courage in particular, and explore the way in which courage stands as part of the larger rounded character to which we are all called. This will set the stage, finally, for some more particular reflections on the way this character manifests itself, as my title suggests, in both peace and war.

Virtue and its embodiment

In my book on Virtue (*Virtue Reborn*, whose US title is *After You Believe*), I have taken as a classic example of 'virtue' a dramatic incident that occurred in January 2009. A plane took off from La Guardia airport in New York City, and ran straight into a flock of Canada Geese. As both engines failed on Flight 1549, the pilot, Chesley Sullenberger III, realized at once that he had to land again, but also that his options were quickly reduced to the worst one: landing in the Hudson River. In two minutes flat he and his co-pilot performed dozens, perhaps hundreds, of small but significant tasks, shutting down some systems and activating others, swinging the plane round in a steep arc, then tipping back to slow down before coming forwards again but not too far, and finally achieving a safe landing. The pilot then walked to and fro through the plane, which was filling up with water, checking that everyone was safely off, before giving his shirt to a passenger who was in particular distress from the biting cold.

Some people at the time called it a 'miracle'. Well, I never want to rule out such things. God moves in mysterious ways. But I think sometimes our culture reaches for the category of 'miracle' because we haven't wanted to face the challenge of character, of virtue. What happened that day was the result of over thirty years of training, teaching, and sheer regular practice. Sullenberger didn't have to stop to think what to do. He didn't have to look it up in a book or ask advice. It was, as we say, 'in his bones'. It 'came naturally'. He wasn't born with this gift. He acquired it by steady, deliberate application.

This story may help to give us a handle on the four mainstream theories about how practical ethics actually works. Much of our culture today gets stuck somewhere between the first three. I believe that focusing on virtue and character marks an important way forward. But first, a quick word about each of the first three.

The first way is the way of Rules. For many people – this, perhaps, is how many people imagine things work in a military context – there is a list of rules, of do's and don'ts. You just have to learn the rules and then force yourself to do them come what may; and wherever you are in a chain of command, unless you are at the very top (and even then you answer to your political masters), you are simply required to obey orders. Blind obedience to arbitrary commands: well, perhaps sometimes life in a military context may feel like that, especially when it's the politicians giving the commands, but for most people today that seems a dehumanized way of going about things. The anti-authoritarian mood of the Western world over the last generation, which is in part a long reaction against totalitarianism, has resulted in a deep suspicion of rules. They smack of a detached, uncaring authority unrelated to the real aspirations and inclinations of those who are supposed to obey them. Our world has lurched towards a thoroughgoing relativism, in which what's true for me may not be true for you, and that includes codes of behaviour, too. Who wants a police officer on each corner, checking up on you all the time?

Part of the answer is, of course, that if there are murderers and rapists around we suddenly *would* like a police officer on each corner. There are limits. Indeed, when it comes to rules, we go on clinging to some of them (rules against child-abuse or genocide, for instance), and we actually become quite shrill about them, partly because there are not many left, so our moral energy gets focused on the few remaining ones.

Anyway: the first and perhaps best known and obvious ethical system is that of rules; and many people today find it sadly deficient as an account of either genuine morality or good practical action. If Chesley Sullenberger had had to look up the rules for what to do in an emergency, the plane would have crashed long before he'd checked the index for 'goose strike' and found the right page.

The second option, at the other pole, is the principle of 'doing what comes naturally'. For many people today, that is the only real rule. A few years ago I came across a sign, in a junk shop on the California coast, which said, 'There are times I think I'm doing things on principle; but mostly I just do what feels good; but that's a principle too.' The cult of 'spontaneity' grew up in the nineteenth century in reaction to the high-and-dry culture of 'rules', in an attempt to involve the person at a much deeper level. It has acquired extra impetus from some more recent movements which have emphasized the need for 'authenticity', being true to oneself.

The problem with this should be obvious. Left to ourselves, many of us would be lazy, fickle, spendthrift and unreliable – to say nothing of worse. That is what 'comes naturally'. People have sometimes tried to justify such behaviour by saying that they were doing what they most felt like at the time. But, however much we may want to avoid going back to a mere rule-based morality, most people, upon reflection, would conclude that 'spontaneity' or 'authenticity' won't do as a complete account of how the moral life should work. Again, if the pilot in the plane had been a novice who simply decided to 'do what comes naturally', disaster would have been guaranteed.

The best-known attempt to carve a path between dry 'rules' on the one hand and self-centred 'spontaneity' on the other has been the third option, 'utilitarianism' or 'consequentialism'. This is the belief that the morality of an act can be assessed by its consequences, and that one always ought to aim at the result of the greatest happiness of the greatest number. This sounds fine in theory, but as soon as you try it in practice, particularly in really difficult moral situations, it won't do. You can't possibly calculate the multiple unforeseen outcomes of any action, great or small. Even if we confine ourselves to the outcomes we can see, it's often a hard call. In tricky practical or moral situations our mental calculus is likely to be swayed by self-interest or prejudice. What's more, by itself the distant goal of 'happiness' doesn't tell us much about the intermediate stages you need to get there. Obviously, the pilot of Flight 1549 was hoping to maximize the happiness of everyone both on board and on the ground. But that intention alone wouldn't have been enough to save the plane.

The fourth route is the one I want to commend: that of 'virtue'. A virtue-approach attempts to have the best of all worlds – though, because virtue means hard work, it is often sidelined. Rules still matter, because they act as the guidelines which indicate whether the virtues are indeed present, and as the guard-rails which stop those whose virtue is as yet limited from going off the road altogether. But a virtue-ethic insists not so much on rules, but on the development of particular strengths of character. 'Strength', as we saw, is what the Latin word *virtus* means. You develop the virtue of justice in the same way that you develop a particular muscle, by exercising it, or in the way you develop a particular mental ability – say, doing mental arithmetic or learning a language – by practising it. Eventually, the muscle that used to get tired and stiff quite quickly is able to do the exercise without noticing it. Eventually, working out complex sums in your head, or speaking Russian fluently, is something you do without stopping to think. So with virtue: when you have thought through, for instance, what 'justice' really means, and concentrated on acting in accordance with it for months and years, it becomes part of your personality. It is stamped into you. It is (that is) part of your 'character'.

At this point, the first two systems have combined into something much greater than either of them, greater, too, than the sum of their parts. When you become fluent in the language, you stop thinking about the rules of grammar, not because you're getting them all wrong but because you're getting them all right. At the same point, you are not forcing yourself to do something peculiar, or, as we say, out of 'character'. You have had to do a lot of that kind of hard work on the way to the destination, just like someone going into training for an athletics event. But now you're doing what comes naturally – naturally, that is, for someone who's done all the hard work up front. And whereas utilitarianism would require you, under the sudden pressure of a moral or practical dilemma, to make complex calculations containing lots of unknowns, virtue has done the calculations long ago, and trusts that the unknowns will look after themselves. What we have, in short, is the acquired facility – I had almost said the acquired taste – for acting in a particular way: the ingrained habit that makes particular patterns of life, thought, feeling and action appear natural, even though, to begin with, they may have been anything but.

This is why virtue is often spoken of as 'second nature'. We are not born with the natural ability to do justice, to behave with prudence, or to control and curb our natural instincts, any more than we are born with the ability to fly a plane, let alone to land one without engines on a wintry river. But we acquire this 'second nature' by *making choices*: by thinking it through, in other words, by determining that we shall act in a particular way, and by learning those habits much as one learns a musical instrument or a foreign language. Here is a key difference between virtue and vice. Vice can be, just as much as virtue, a fixed habit of the heart, something that has you in its grip. But to acquire a vice requires no effort, no thought, no reflection, no act of will. All you have to do is go with the flow into whatever bad habits your temperament may lead you. That is another reason why the cult of spontaneity – doing what comes naturally – is such a poor way of ordering one's life.

So how do we tell what character-traits are the appropriate virtues to cultivate? It all depends on your goal. For Aristotle, the goal – he used the word *telos* – was 'happiness', *eudaimonia*, not in the casual sense we might use to describe our feelings after a nice cup of tea or a cheerful movie, but in the much deeper sense of a rich human satisfaction arrived at when we find ourselves to be fully alive and fully functioning. In fact, what we mean by 'happiness' has changed over time, and with shifts in culture. Part of the challenge for us today, in peace as well as in war, has to do with a fresh glimpse of the goals we should be setting ourselves right across Western society, and then the character-strengths we need to develop in order to come at those goals. To this I shall return.

During the research I have undertaken on this subject, I have been fascinated by the evidence that one's character and habits of life may have to do quite literally with changes in the brain. Studies of London taxi-drivers indicate that the hippocampus, the part of the brain that does spatial reasoning, is significantly larger, actually *physically* larger, than in the rest of the population. Every time we make a choice or act in a particular way, it seems, we create or develop neural pathways in our brains which make it more 'natural' to behave in the same way again. As the habit develops, not only will it seem 'natural'. It will make it hard to remember, or even to imagine, what it was like when it wasn't 'natural'.

It is perhaps an alarming thought that our behaviour, even in what we think of as casual speech and action, leaves tracks through our brains like the electronic traces in a computer's memory. But the positive side of this is vital, I suggest, not only for moral theory – that the aim of all moral teaching is to produce human beings who do the right thing by second nature, without having to stop and think about it as they used to have to do – but also for the severely practical side of life, whether it be fighting a war or building a house, running a care home or writing a book. I suspect that those in the military know better than most of us the need to develop what we call 'instinctive' behaviour (though, again, we would have to call it 'second instinct', since nobody does these things naturally from birth or without training). Those involved in war above all are required to face unexpected challenges and problems which give them no time to stop and think. To be sure, there will usually be time to think through and discuss wider strategic choices. But when battle is joined there is no time to look up the answer in a book, or to debate the matter for a couple of days and take a vote. There will certainly be no chance to investigate and ponder all the possible consequences of this or that course of action.

Many today might be shocked to learn what follows from this. The armed forces may have had to preserve in our culture a truth which has far wider implications and applications: that a full, genuine human life is found not by blindly following rules but by becoming the sort of person who acts in the right way *because that's the sort of person they have become* through the sheer slog of character-building. That process of 'becoming' inevitably means hard work, difficult choices stuck to through gritted teeth, a steep uphill pattern of learning and training. This is deeply unwelcome in our present culture of 'spontaneity' or 'authenticity'. But it is so necessary for that different, higher kind of spontaneity and authenticity we call 'second nature'.

One more word of initial exposition. It seems to me that the pilot of Flight 1459, Chesley Sullenberger, exhibited all four of what Aristotle called the 'cardinal virtues': courage, justice, temperance and prudence. Courage, obviously: cool under intense and immediate danger, determined to put everyone else's safety before his own. Justice: he was automatically determined to give to everyone, including innocent civilians on the ground, their proper due. Temperance: he must have restrained all kinds of natural impulses, keeping himself well under control. And prudence: he was able to think through the options available to him at lightning speed and to make the right choice. As Aristotle and others saw, for any of these virtues to exist, you actually need all four, and probably more ancillary ones beside. They belong together and reinforce one another.

My basic proposal about the nature of virtue, then, is that the steady, hard-working, chosen and intentional development of character offers a far more satisfying picture of how the human being can become most fully what he or she was made to be than the other regular accounts. In particular, this account of virtue shows up rather starkly the two currently popular alternatives, the first two models I mentioned earlier. These may be thought of, broadly, as the left-wing and right-wing viewpoints. On the left, we have the cult of spontaneity and authenticity: doing what feels good, being true to yourself, not letting fuddy-duddy old rules cramp your style. That's a recipe for a free-floating semi-anarchic lifestyle, and the trouble with anarchy is that the bullies and the loudmouths tend to win. In any case, even the free-floating left-wing spontaneity can't actually do without its own new rules: witness (for instance) the rise of the new and rather fierce ecological taboos about recycling and alternative sources of energy. I happen to approve of both of those (though I have questions about some of the alternative sources).

But my point is the ironic one: in the UK in the early years of the twenty-first century it was precisely a Labour government, committed in theory to 'freedom' in all directions, that introduced more fussy, wrist-slapping rules and regulations than any other government in our history. Sadly, governments have few philosophers to argue out their strategies. If they did, that government might have realized that it was balancing out the futility of trying to make everyone free with the futility of trying to make everyone good by statute. Plato knew the answer to that: education. It has been left to such educationalists as still believe in it, and to such institutions as the military and some other professions, to work at the character development which should have been the priority all along.

On the right, however, we have the fierce rule-based moralism of those who see the danger of the left's shoulder-shrugging anarchy.

This is more apparent at the moment in the USA than the UK, but there may be many on both sides of the Atlantic who yearn for a more ordered world, for a chance to put the genie of liberalism back into the bottle and to return to being the somewhat regimented but basically peaceful and ordered society we remember, or at least imagine. Again, it can't be done; and the good news is that it doesn't need to be thought of like that. Once more, we need education. If the schools can't or won't provide the development of character and virtue, then, as before, it's up to the professions, not least the armed forces, to provide it instead. But it must be provided precisely *as* character-forming and character-transforming education, not simply (as in the caricature) a matter of irrational orders blindly obeyed. Give people some fish, and you feed them for a day; teach people to fish and you feed them for life. Give people an order and you shape their behaviour for as long as it takes to obey. Teach people virtue and you shape their behaviour for life.

The question then is, of course: how can you do that?

Let me then turn to examine the notion of courage, as one of the key virtues. What is it, and how does it work?

Courage among the virtues

It isn't too hard to say what we mean by 'courage'. In fact, it's considerably easier than identifying justice, temperance or prudence. I recall a sermon in Westminster Abbey by the then Archbishop of Canterbury, Rowan Williams, when dedicating the memorial to holders of the Victoria Cross. He distinguished sharply between the person who takes a strong drink and charges into battle shouting a war-cry and waving a sword around, on the one hand, and on the other hand the person who calmly makes a thousand small decisions to put someone else's safety ahead of his or her own and then, on the thousand and first occasion, does so instinctively, without thought, because courage has become a habit of the heart. There we see the two key points. First, genuine courage must be distinguished from mere crazy daring or foolhardy risk-taking, fuelled perhaps by what we unwisely call 'Dutch courage' (I wonder what they call it in Holland?). Second, the road to that genuine courage is the voluntary, thought-out and perhaps hard-won choice of a consistent pattern of behaviour which becomes a habit, not just a one-off random act.

What we observe in the case of genuine courage, in fact, is bravery in the service of, and having been moderated by, the other three cardinal virtues, justice, temperance and prudence. Here I retrace the steps of Aristotle and many others, but in today's idiom and context.

First, courage is bravery *in the service of justice*. There is no point in doing dangerous things just for the sake of it – though I suppose there may be something to be said for sports like rock climbing, which teach you to balance not only your body but also the qualities of bravery and self-preservation. True courage is bravery in the service of giving to each their due, that is, justice. That can be seen in those remarkable civilian examples, such as the heroic bravery of the man in a sinking ferry who turned his own body into a bridge so that people could walk across him and escape to safety. It is also, without a doubt, on display daily in various theatres of war, not least among those who calmly dismantle bombs so that others may not be blown up by them. It may perhaps also be visible when people speak out with genuine courage to restate unpopular truths, giving to wider society a vision of justice (for instance, on behalf of asylum-seekers) while incurring opprobrium from those who follow the popular mood. And if genuine courage is bravery in the service of justice, it must also be bravery *tempered by* justice. We shall return to this presently when thinking about appropriate courage in war.

But if genuine courage is bravery in the pursuit of giving to others what is their due – in these cases, safety and welfare – it is also bravery *moderated by temperance*. That is, it must be a bravery which expresses self-control rather than self-seeking or self-serving. As members of the military will know better than I do, the genuine hero is unlikely to think of him- or herself as a hero at all. Heroes are too busy thinking about the other people whose safety is their primary concern. They do what they do through controlling and restraining the self and its impulses, rather than through the hunger for personal celebrity or glory. Quite often those who are decorated for great bravery seem genuinely puzzled: they were simply doing what had to be done. But the bravery consists precisely in the character-strength of knowing what had to be done and getting on and doing it, when most people would either panic or make themselves scarce, or both. And true courage will, almost by definition, also be bravery *in the service of* temperance: that is, true courage promotes self-control, restraining the natural impulse for self-preservation, for one's own comfort and security, in order that one may serve the preservation, comfort and security of others.

Obviously, once again, in many spheres of human activity, not least in military service, individual acts of courage may well be made at several removes from their hoped-for effects. There are the times when one soldier instinctively throws himself as a human shield between the grenade that is about to explode and the group of civilians who will be killed unless he gets in the way. But there are also the times when the soldier has to trust that the act of courage he or she has to undertake here and now will in fact be for the good of others, even though that equation only makes sense in the light of the larger presuppositions on which the entire war is being fought.

Courage, then, belongs with justice and temperance; and also, clearly, with prudence. There is no point in performing acts of bravery as it were at random, for example fording a dangerous river when there is no advantage in attaining the other bank, or defusing a bomb in an area no-one is ever likely to visit. Prudence puts an appropriate brake on courage, and prevents it from lapsing into mere risky foolhardiness. But courage must also be *in the service of* prudence. I think of Desmond Tutu standing in front of an angry and potentially violent mob, and explaining to them the virtues of peaceful protest and patience. Tutu won out in the end, but it took massive courage, risking not only verbal abuse but also personal danger from extremists, in order to advocate that prudence, that moderation. It is easy to see, then, that genuine courage belongs with the other three cardinal virtues, and indeed is held in place by them.

The 'cardinal virtues' are common to many ethical traditions, going back to ancient Greece. But I also want to suggest that genuine courage is also a feature of the more specifically Christian virtue-set, and is a goal to be aimed at with all the resources of Christian spiritual discipline. The Bible, after all, includes plenty of commands to be courageous. These go back at least as far as God's commands to Joshua before the entry into the promised land (Joshua 1.6, etc.), and come all the way through to Jesus' commands to his followers to be courageous because he had already conquered the world (John 16.33). Likewise, Paul commands the Corinthians to 'Keep alert; stand firm in the faith; be courageous; be strong; let all that you do be done in love' (1 Corinthians 16.13). That last set of commands makes perfectly the point I want to draw out: that from the Christian point of view courage is required to witness to Jesus Christ in a hostile world, and that courage is held in place by hope ('keep alert', a command closely related to the Christian expectation of God's coming great future), by the faith in which one is to stand firm, and by the love that is to characterize one's every action.

One of the key differences between Christian virtue and Aristotelian virtue comes in here. For Aristotle, the virtues are all about the great and often lonely individual. For the Christian they are a team sport. Far too often the practice of Christian faith is seen, both by insiders and by outsiders, in terms of the individual making his or her way to heaven and trying to behave appropriately en route. In that context, 'courage' can be reduced to my courage in speaking unpopular truths from the pulpit, your courage in refusing to join in with questionable conversation among your colleagues, or bad behaviour after hours, or someone else's courage in saying his or her prayers within the unavoidably public and visible world of a battle-unit. Those things matter; but actually the courage which is demanded of the Christian goes far beyond that.

Like all courage, specifically Christian courage consists in the resolute determination to put other people's safety and well-being ahead of your own. More particularly, though, it cherishes a vision of God and God's kingdom according to which there is a battle going on, with the initial victory of Jesus Christ pointing forwards to the final victory in which death itself will be defeated and God will be all in all. Christian courage is the settled habit of heart, mind and life through which we always keep those two victories in sight, and in which we put ourselves at the disposal of God and of our fellow humans in the service of that final victory, whatever it may cost. The only way one can do that is by being part of the team, that is, the church; and by understanding oneself not as acting alone but as playing one's proper role within a huge army, where each person is given his or her own bit of the field on which to operate. Courage, in the Christian sense, thus takes its place within the larger picture of Christian character sketched in the New Testament, following Jesus in the power of the Spirit.

I hope it is clear from all this that 'courage' in the wider sense, and 'courage' in the more specifically Christian sense, are not two different things. They flow into and out of one another. That points us to the larger proposal I want to outline in the third and final section of this chapter.

Courage in peace and war

A good deal of both the classical and the Christian vision of courage applies quite naturally and obviously to the practice of war. Those in the military are the experts on that, and will have their own favourite examples of genuine courage on the battlefield. But I want to suggest that this somewhat specialized setting of courage belongs closely with, and informs importantly, the courage we need at this moment in our Western society. Let me explain.

We live at a peculiar moment in the developing story of Western culture. The modernist movement, stemming from the European Enlightenment of the eighteenth century, swept away many previous certainties. Democracy replaced autocracy, and frequently this came about by violence. Modern science and historiography questioned what had seemed fixed religious truths. Instead of an earlier humility before the vastness of the universe, humankind declared itself to be the measure of all things, able to find out ultimate truth and manipulate it to serve its own purposes. Unfortunately, the modernist experiment reached its climax with Hitler, Stalin and Mao Zedong. That is partly at least why the cynical questioning which modernism applied to previously held certainties has for the last generation been applied to modernism itself, in what is sometimes called postmodernism. In this movement, which has affected everything from architecture to advertising, there are no fixed truths at all. We bend all reality to our wills, though our wills themselves are constantly changing. There are no great stories left to guide us, whether the ancient ones of the religions or the modern one of ever-greater Progress. One of the slogans for this is Deconstruction.

We all know this crisis-moment in our culture, because we have all lived at the heart of it, even if we haven't given it a name. In 2001 the world shuddered as Deconstruction came out of the shadows of theory and became a horrible fact, with the postmodern weapon of terrorism smashing two symbols of high modernism, the World Trade Center and the Pentagon. We responded, it seems to me, in a highly questionable way, using the traditional warfare of modernism – tanks and bombs – to go after an enemy playing by different and essentially postmodern rules, in terrain, and under sociological conditions, for which the modernist warfare developed in Europe is (to put it mildly) less than fully suitable. (We also seem to have gone after the wrong enemy in the wrong place; that is another story.) Part of the problem here, I think, is that for the Western powers, particularly the USA, it is literally unthinkable that high modernism should not be able to defeat all comers. The United States is the archetypal modernist project. If you question that, you shake the foundations.

What is more, we have ignored the irreducible and highly complex religious dimension of almost all the trouble-spots in the world. We have assumed, in classic modernist fashion, that religion is an outdated, dangerous noise on the surface of a culture, and that for practical purposes, whether good or ill, it is best to ignore it. In all this we have been urged down the wrong path by the media, who continue to use all the language and rhetoric of modernism (invoking 'progress' at every turn and ignoring the religious dimension), and who love to look down on religion from the supposed high ground of sophisticated scepticism while constantly playing the card of postmodern relativism with its spin, smear and innuendo. This, too, is no doubt familiar territory. Most people, however, know in their bones that there are spiritual dimensions to life, and that they integrate with everything else. We ignore that at our peril; or, rather, we have ignored it and now face the peril. As I am editing this chapter for publication (14 November 2015), news has arrived of a terrorist attack in Paris which makes this point in a horribly graphic fashion.

My suggestion here is that it is time to turn the page, to start a new chapter, to sketch a different and more integrated worldview and to live from within it. The idea of a 'secular' society, with 'religion' either privatized or marginalized, simply won't do. Pragmatically, it doesn't fit almost any actual country in the world – certainly not the UK, where at the last census 59 per cent of the population described themselves as 'Christian'. (That was significantly down on the previous figure, but it is still a solid majority.) But it goes beyond that. The very idea of a separation of the 'secular' from the 'religious', with the two then needing to talk to one another, is itself a thoroughly modernist idea which is long past its sell-by date. Somehow we have to work at the hard and sometimes dangerous task of articulating, and living by, a worldview in which faith and public life are appropriately integrated.

This is anything but an airy-fairy philosophical discussion. It concerns real people, hard decisions, bones and blood, facts on the ground. And that integration, I believe, should be our new goal, our contemporary *telos*. As you recall, the virtues are defined in relation to the goal: they are the strengths of character that, you might say, are borrowed from that future, or are training us to be at home in that future. My point in saying all this, of course, is that such work takes courage; and it takes a courage which has been redefined in relation to this redefinition of the wider societal task we face today. The courage we need in these urgent tasks is itself the anticipation of the integrated humanness we seek.

It takes courage to pursue this agenda because there are plenty of people around, including those with media platforms, and many in politics, for whom any attempt to re-integrate faith and public life is anathema. They will loudly object to any such proposal. Sometimes this is because they have been bruised early on by religious teaching or upbringing, and they have spent their lives reacting against it. Sometimes it's because they rejected one particular aspect of what their priest, their pastor, their rabbi or their imam had taught them; and they then reject the whole structure in order to justify their original protest. Sometimes, naturally, objections arise from a thought-out philosophical or political position. But the kind of objectors I am talking about have loud voices, and they are masters of the long sneer. They claim the high moral ground and look down their noses at those of us who articulate a different vision. And if you are going to be part of that new movement of speaking and living by that different dream, of a fresh integration of faith and life, you will need courage: not foolhardiness, speaking rashly or intemperately, but calm, confident courage.

It takes courage to glimpse a different vision or reality, to live it and, as opportunity affords, to speak it. Here I'm not sure that I can get a razor blade between the 'ordinary' type of courage and the 'Christian' variety. That is symptomatic of the very point I'm making, that it is time to bring faith and public life, classical virtue and Christian virtue, together. This, I suggest, is the courage we need all the time, the courage to which we are all called at this moment in Western society. Peace should be seen as a gift which allows us the leisure to think out our worldviews more wisely than before. As we do that, we will need to speak with clarity and courage.

If that is the courage we require today in peace, the courage required in war is not so very different. Undoubtedly, there are specific skills and contexts which are peculiar to battle. But the virtue of courage is vital at every stage. We have heard a lot over the years about 'just war theory', divided into *jus in bello*, the question of how to behave with justice during the actual fighting, and *jus ad bellum*, the question of whether it is just to go to war in the first place. We could ask the same questions in relation to courage. We might take it for granted that one needs courage *in bello*, during actual fighting. I hope what I said earlier is borne in mind here, that true courage is correlated with justice, temperance and prudence, and is best maintained through faith, hope and love. I do not think, as some do, that this is a contradiction in terms, or that Christians are automatically committed to pacifism. Rulers have a responsibility to protect the weak and vulnerable, and when there are violent bullies around they must be restrained. War is thus a form of police action, a necessary evil granted the way the world still is. The ingrained habit of courage is required at every level to undertake this kind of action.

It seems to me, looking on from the sidelines as neither a policeman nor a soldier, that this is all the more necessary in a military world where, because of new technology, every soldier is far more aware than any previous generation has been of the multiple dimensions of what is going on. It is no longer enough, today, to tell the troops to do what they're told and ask no questions. They must be taught the virtues which will enable them to think and act with mature responsibility.

But what about courage *ad bellum*, in the approach to war itself? We have, of course, a clear and worrying recent example of a war undertaken largely because the politicians in the UK and USA were keen on it even though they hadn't thought it through (and even though many thought then, and think still, that it was not only unwise but illegal). Various military leaders, who at the time did what the politicians told them to, have said subsequently that the reasons for going to war, and the plans for what to do next, were, to say the least, deficient. I have pondered the question of how military leaders can discern when they have reached the point at which the truly courageous thing is for the leaders of the armed forces to tell the politicians that they've got it wrong, and perhaps to do so publicly, recognizing that such a move would take courage bordering on foolhardiness in terms of one's own career. Perhaps that is the moral equivalent of the person who throws himself on the grenade to prevent it killing the children nearby. Alternatively, there may be times – who knows what new situations we are going to face in the coming days? – when military leaders have to tell our civilian leaders that the security of the realm demands that we *do* go to war, even when the politicians, for whatever reason, don't wish to do so or haven't seen the danger coming. Again, this will take great courage. I suspect that this sort of courage *ad bellum* may be just as tough as courage *in bello*. One can envisage a comparable situation in terms of the forming and maintaining of a wise policy about possessing, or not possessing, a nuclear deterrent.

In all this, then, I am assuming that those who are called to exercise courage in peace and in war are called to develop it as a habit of the heart, as a 'virtue' in the sense I described earlier, as a facet of one's deepest character. We urgently need leaders who have developed this habit from their early days, and have learned how to balance it with justice, temperance and prudence, and indeed with faith, hope and love. And 'courage' is nothing if not embodied. It regularly demands that you go calmly into a situation which, left to yourself, you would much rather not face, whether it be to drive a jeep along a bomb-infested road, to rescue a wounded comrade under fire, or even to face a hostile Committee.

How do you teach all that without creating dangerously artificial situations which can be exploited by bullies? I suspect that a good part of it is sheer example, both direct and through military history and biography; and also being part of a team where everyone encourages, and is encouraged by, their neighbours. The very word 'encourage' indicates that this may be partly at least how it works.

Conclusion

I have tried to outline what virtue is and why it matters, and particularly what courage is and why we urgently need it today. The old divisions of sacred and secular, of religion and public life, have outlived any usefulness they had. We therefore live in a strange new world which many of our contemporaries don't like and don't want – a world in which, just as faith and politics cannot actually be separated, so too the classical virtues need to be integrated with those that spring from faith. But it is, I believe, a world full of hope and new possibilities. To glimpse this hope, and to grasp these possibilities, will take courage. Those who have learned that virtue in war may well be called to use it in peace. Those of us who struggle to practise courage in articulating and living the Christian worldview against the continuing cynicism of the postmodern world are grateful for their example.

9

Christian faith in public life

'God in the Dock' is the title of a short essay by C. S. Lewis, which was then used as the title of a collection of such works. The pithy pieces that make up that collection are Lewis at his best, arguing a coherent case for the truth of the Christian faith and the reasonableness of belief. The title 'God in the Dock' comes from Lewis's observation that secular modernism, instead of regarding God as the judge before whom we must all stand, has reversed the scenario. God himself is in the dock, with our culture providing prosecution, judge and jury.

What Lewis would have said had he seen today's judges and jurors it is daunting to guess. Lewis imagined his modernist judges to be quite kindly. They were, he says, ready to hear a case for the defence, and might even acquit God of his apparent crimes. Not so the New Atheists of our own day. They stridently accuse God of everything imaginable and allow him no excuses, no defence. Reading people like Richard Dawkins, I am reminded of Kingsley Amis's famous remark when someone asked him if he believed in God. 'No,' he replied, 'and I hate him.' There is a level of raw anger in some of the recent writing which, as many commentators have pointed out, makes the claim to be representing the humanist principle of reason somewhat hard to sustain.

These attacks have brought into sharp public focus certain questions which have been rumbling along in Western culture for well over a couple of centuries, and which are now facing us with a new kind of force. I want to get at them in the present chapter – which was originally a lecture given in Dublin, and the specifically Irish focus will come through at various points – by sketching three stories, three narratives, the first two of which are well enough known but the third of which is less so. It won't surprise you that I am using the familiar trick of setting up two positions, neither of which I find satisfactory, and offering a third which is not a compromise between them so much as a different kind of story altogether.

The secularist thesis

I lived for five years in the Canadian province of Quebec. Quebec remained traditionally and vibrantly Roman Catholic while the rest of America embraced the Enlightenment. Then, almost overnight in the 1970s, it decided it didn't believe that stuff any more, and pursued a vigorous secularization in all areas of life. The dogged and unquestioning loyalty formerly given to the church was then given instead to the *Parti Québécois*; but that, too, has now been variously discredited and debunked, leaving Quebec puzzled, as the rest of us are, with the ambiguities of modern democracy and economics.

But my point is this. Underneath the slow erosion of the older ways that has taken place in Europe since the middle of the eighteenth century, and underneath the much more rapid erosion that has taken place in Quebec, Ireland and elsewhere, there lies a set of beliefs about the world which we can loosely call secular modernism. It tells a consistent story which goes like this. Once upon a time the world was dominated by religion. This caused all kinds of superstition, with people ascribing to supernatural causes phenomena (thunderstorms, epilepsy, and plenty of other things), which are now explained by science. Superstitious religion produced all kinds of wickedness, as the church sought to order and regulate the lives of individuals and whole societies while continuing itself to amass power, to hoard wealth, and – despite protestations of chastity – to tolerate undercover sexual licence. In fact (so runs the secularist thesis) religion, not least the Christian religion and its Catholic manifestation, has been responsible for many of the major ills in the world, for wars, crusades and inquisitions, for the repression of women and the abuse of children. The church has made people's lives hell in the present, in the belief that they were thereby rescuing them from hell in the future.

In fact (concludes the secularist in triumph), we now know that all this is nonsense. Modern science has disproved God, miracles, heaven and hell, the whole lot. Modern history has undermined the old stories about Jesus, particularly his resurrection. Modern politics has shown us that democracy is far better than the old unchallenged divine right of popes and kings. And modern sociology, anthropology and psychology have shown us that human beings are burdened neither with being in the image of 'god' nor with 'original sin'. What they need is education, science, technology and – just now at least – a better economic climate. Then we can all thrive together. Meanwhile the Whig view of history applies to society and morals as to everything else: 'progress' is still under way, things are getting more liberal, more open, more free, and 'now that we live in the twenty-first century' we have to say farewell to all those old superstitions and restrictive moral codes, and welcome the brave new world where 'human rights' means that everyone has the right to do whatever they like. The recent appalling acts of religiously motivated terrorists, declares the secularist, have only uncovered what was there all along: a little religion goes a long way – in entirely the wrong direction.

I caricature only a little. This narrative, or something quite like it, has dominated public discourse in England and Scotland most of my life, getting more strident as it has gone on. Our national media take this for granted as their starting-point. Now, I understand, something similar has become more common in Ireland as well. It is assumed that religion in general and Christianity in particular is out of date, disproved, bad for your health, the cause of many great evils. And it is assumed that the church, as well as peddling this evil thing, is internally corrupt, hypocritical, and unfit for anything except the scrapbook of history. To the question, then, whether Christian faith now has any place in public life, the secularist responds with a resounding 'No'. Voltaire's motto has come home to roost: *Écrasez l'infame*, 'Wipe out the disgrace'. Clear the church and its monstrous teaching off the scene, and we shall build a new kind of new Jerusalem by our own efforts instead. Thus, whenever the church tries to say anything today in the public square, loud voices are raised to tell it to shut up. I know this from my experience in the House of Lords; the same thing was seen in Ireland when, for instance, the Catholic bishops tried to oppose the bill to legalize 'civil partnerships'. According to this first story, things are getting easier because the churches are in any case being edged out of the reckoning. They are emptying of their own accord, and being sold off for use as homes, wine bars and warehouses. Fairly soon nothing will be left except a nostalgic and increasingly elderly remnant.

The older story revived?

My second story is, I take it, a fairly normal Christian response. Most Christians will agree that the church has made mistakes. But although some churches are emptying, others are filling, not only in Africa, Latin America and South-East Asia, not only in China, but in our own islands. As a prediction of what would happen, the secularist prophecy has failed. And the intellectual charges of the New Atheists have been refuted, point by point, by writers such as Alister McGrath and David Bentley Hart. What's more, several have pointed out that many of the worst crimes against humanity have been committed, not by Christians or indeed Muslims, but by the children of the Enlightenment, the atheistic or even downright pagan Nazis on the one hand and the avowedly atheist Marxists of China and the Soviet Union on the other. The founding heroes of secular modernism, the French Revolutionaries, got rid of the 'infamy' all right, but they got rid of one another too, at quite an alarming rate. As we saw in an earlier chapter, the guillotine and the gas chamber are two of secular modernism's most potent and revealing symbols. If this is 'progress', as C. S. Lewis pointed out, it is the kind you see in an egg: 'We call it "going bad" in Narnia,' declares Prince Caspian.

What's more, reply the traditionalists quite rightly, one needs to distinguish good religion from bad. Christians, Muslims and Jews, after all, got on more or less all right as neighbours in the Middle East for hundreds of years. The strident terrorism of recent decades is almost entirely a 'modern' phenomenon, even in some senses a postmodern one.

But the story which the Christian respondents have been telling has, by and large, not really addressed – so far as I am aware – the deeper question of whether there is therefore any place for Christian faith in public life. Nor has it addressed, I think, the question which is urgent in Ireland right now, the question of how on earth the church not only perpetrated such massive and horrible abuse but then did its best to cover it up. I am not sure that those who want to tell the second story have really come to grips with the sheer cold fury expressed by the Irish Prime Minister in 2011 when he spoke out on behalf of millions of ordinary people against what was widely seen as a serious failure on the part of the church.

Perhaps all this is why a good deal of the response to the first story has simply concentrated on rebutting the charge that Christianity is disproved or bad for you, leaving the Christianity that is thereby defended as basically a private faith, which the church can then proclaim, and people can believe, with integrity and good reason. Much of the defence has assumed, it seems to me, that when we have seen off the newer challenges we can resume business as normal – a bit like the banks after the credit crunch. And I hold the view that what was 'normal' for the Christian churches in the Western world after the Enlightenment is not in fact 'normal' by the canons of classic Christianity. We need to revisit the larger, underlying questions, and not assume that the way we were functioning before was basically all right once we'd cleaned up a few small details. That, in fact, is how the church has often been perceived: covering up mistakes or imagining that they can be parked to one side, allowing the main business to proceed without noticing serious cracks in the structure. The twin dangers of nostalgia and complacency are always with us. However effective the church's answers to the New Atheists may be in theory, this does not absolve us from thinking afresh, first about just how the church allowed itself to get into the mess in the first place, and second (and only when we have worked through the first question) about how a healthy Christian faith and life might impinge upon public life in our world and our day.

The first question is important, but I'm not sure I have the competence to deal with it. My hunch is that the church has, over many generations, allowed itself simultaneously to do two things. First, it has colluded with the Enlightenment proposal that Christianity is simply about 'religion' and 'morality' – but since 'morality' has been such a contested area, and since in any case one can always repent afterwards, a slow decline in actual moral standards has taken place, accelerated by the liberalism of the 1960s. Second, in many churches, not least but not only the Roman church, ordination or its equivalent has been supposed to put people on a new kind of level, so that 'ordinary' Christians find it hard to believe ill of the clergy, and so that they themselves, and their superiors, tend to assume that any moral failings are an odd blip rather than a major character defect. All churches, and all clergy, need to look hard in the mirror at this point.

Only then, with genuine penitence, can we address the possibility of Christian faith and public life. Here I will inevitably stand against the tide. To an outsider it looks as though Ireland is at last plugging into the anti-Christian, anti-Catholic and anti-clerical reaction which Voltaire articulated and which has dominated much of the rest of Europe, not to mention America. Scandals in the church on the one hand, and the ostensible 'religious' alignments in 'the troubles' to the north, make all this much worse, but I don't think that is the underlying problem.

Whether or not I am right about that, it is time to move to my third narrative. I want to propose a way of looking at the role of Christian faith in public life which is not well known. Even to articulate it requires us to step back a bit and consider two things: what Jesus and his first followers were actually saying, and what has happened to Western culture – and now finally, it seems, to Ireland where Western Christian culture began in the first place! – in the last few generations.

The kingdom of God and the kingdoms of the world

The third story I wish to tell must begin with Jesus himself. Interestingly, the New Atheists tend to assume that Jesus can be safely discounted as a minor figure whose followers, after his death, invented a few stories about him and a religion around him. Christian apologists, myself included, have responded by saying that actually the stories in the gospels are far more historically reliable than you might think. But we have not usually gone beyond this to a fresh articulation of what was, arguably, central for Jesus: the notion of the kingdom of God.

Here we face a new kind of puzzle. For many Christians it would have been sufficient if Jesus of Nazareth had been born of a virgin and died on a cross, and never done anything much in between. Insofar as the gospels record his deeds and words, these simply function to teach doctrines and ethics we might have learned from Paul or elsewhere. But this characteristic Western misreading of the gospels omits the central point: that Jesus went about announcing *that God was now in charge*, doing things which embodied that in-charge-ness, that sovereignty, that 'kingdom', and telling stories which explained that this divine kingdom was coming, not in the way people were expecting, but like a tiny seed producing a huge shrub, like a father welcoming back a runaway son. All the gospels record that Jesus' public career began with an incident (his baptism) which marked him out as the long-awaited king of Israel. They all record that he died with the words 'king of the Jews' above his head. In the biblical tradition, the expected king of the Jews is the king of the world, the one through whom the creator God will establish his rule across the whole world. That claim is made explicit at the end of Matthew's gospel: all authority, says the risen Jesus, is given to me in heaven *and on earth*. Most Western Christians have been happy to suppose that Jesus now has authority in heaven (whatever that means). Few have even begun to contemplate what it might look like for him to have authority on earth as well.

There are two obvious reasons why this extraordinary claim is usually not even noticed. Both relate directly to the challenge of 'doing God in public', of Christian faith and public life. First, it is unbelievable; second, it is undesirable. First, people in Jesus' own day and ever since have responded to Jesus' own claims and those of his followers by saying that it's obvious the kingdom of God has not arrived. Look out of the window, they say. Read the newspapers. If God was in charge, why is the world still in such a mess? (Naturally, Jesus' followers knew this too, but they went on making the claim.) Second, Western culture has struggled over many centuries to throw off what it sees precisely as *theocracy*, recognizing that when people claim that God's in charge what they normally mean is that *their interpretation of God and his rule* must be given absolute status. The rule of God quickly becomes the rule of the clerics. Today's fundamentalist terrorism has sharpened up our reaction to this idea, but the reaction itself goes back not only to the Enlightenment, not only to the uneasy settlements of the Reformation, but as far back as the Renaissance itself. It is possible, in fact, to represent the history of Western politics as the history of the gradual diminishment of 'theocracy' and its displacement by . . . by what?

Well, there's the problem. There have been two great movements of thought and life in the last two hundred years. Both have had direct results on the church and its place in public life. Most obviously, there have been the movements of revolution, from France in the 1780s to China and Russia in the twentieth century, not to mention the countries of the so-called 'third world' attaining independence from colonial rulers. In some of these movements, notably those of communism, the state is divinized: it becomes the highest good, the supreme value, the ultimate giver of meaning and life. The state *must* therefore be *de jure* atheist, not simply because people happen not to believe in God but because there is no room for God in the structure. Those who persist in believing in God are therefore classified as mad, deranged, a danger to society. There can be no place for the church in public life, and indeed ideally no place for the church at all. The failure of the great revolutionary systems to destroy the church, and the way in which, when Eastern European communism fell, some of the movements of opposition were explicitly Christian, has reduced today's hard left in Europe to head-shaking and head-scratching, but has not produced major new insight.

But, second, there have been the great liberal democracies of the Western world, now ironically regarded by many other countries as the kind of system they wish to aspire to at the very point when they, the democracies, are showing signs of wear and tear. And the point about them that has been made with increasing clarity is that, though they haven't tried to replace God, they have tried to replace the church. In my own country, this happened rather obviously in David Cameron's idea of the 'Big Society', where everyone was supposed to be involved in making things happen in their local communities, in caring for the needy. Historically, of course, this was what the church at its best had always done, founding hospitals and schools and so on, and, recently, launching the hugely successful hospice movement and campaigning for remission of global debt. But the church in the West has by and large colluded with this displacement, and has been content to occupy the new, diminished role marked out for it by the philosophy of the Enlightenment, the role of providing a space for 'religion', somewhere quiet on the side. This is where today's debate about Christian faith in public life must learn to engage.

The Enlightenment, in its various waves, saw itself as finally implementing the Epicurean agenda first glimpsed with the rediscovery of Lucretius early in the fifteenth century, a find every bit as momentous as Martin Luther's rediscovery of St Paul early in the sixteenth. The point about Lucretius (who lived about a hundred years before Jesus) and his Epicureanism was that its foundational idea was the banishing of the gods to a far-away heaven, leaving the world and mortals to get on with their happy business here below, uninterrupted and unimpeded. This became the explicit foundation of the modernist agenda to overthrow superstition and religious authority. Indeed, it was Lucretius's account of the development of civilization and of the 'social contract' that, through thinkers like Hobbes and Rousseau, 'enabled historians and philosophers to free themselves from theist models of the foundations of human society' (*Oxford Classical Dictionary*, 3rd revised edition, p. 890).

Thus, though thinkers in this tradition today like to suggest that their views are the result of modern science, a more profound analysis would reveal that modernist science itself, and also the movement for liberal democracy, have simply presupposed the Epicurean worldview. The gods are gone, and the world of nature on the one hand and the world of human society on the other must evolve under their own steam. This then generates a matching split: as between the gods and the world, so between church and society. The church must get on with God's business, which is redefined as inculcating spirituality in the present and a far-off heavenly salvation in the future, for those who want or believe in such things. But the church, *by definition within the dominant Epicurean worldview*, has no place in society or public life. The overthrow of the old medieval order in the Renaissance, and of the old Catholic order in the Reformation, became the overthrow of the whole Christian order in the Enlightenment.

What I think we may see in Ireland today is what, in a less crisp and more muddled fashion, we have seen in England and Scotland in bits and pieces over many years, namely the sharp and brittle clarity gained from the simple disjunction of heaven and earth, of God's world and our world. This disjunction was not itself the result of, but rather the presupposition for, these great movements of Western thought and life. Charles Darwin didn't invent Darwinism. Lucretius had argued it, elegantly, two thousand years earlier. Biological evolution is one thing; but the idea that there is no creator God involved in this process is something quite different.

The church, however, has been happy to go along with the disjunction of God's world and ours. The seeds of this were planted, I think, in the Middle Ages themselves, through the heavy over-concentration on the afterlife, on Dante's vision of heaven, hell and especially purgatory, and on the vision of the End so brilliantly displayed in

Michelangelo's Sistine Chapel. 'This world is not my home,' sang the African-American spiritual, 'I'm just a-passing through'; but those sentiments merely popularized a vision of 'what really mattered' which had been around for many centuries. And so it was not only the thinkers of the Enlightenment, eager to get on with carving up the world the way they wanted and therefore keen on not having the church telling it what it could and couldn't do, who told the church it should concentrate on God, the soul and heaven. The same message was coming from many within the church itself. That is part of the reason why William Wilberforce had such a hard time in pushing his agenda of freeing the slaves, why Desmond Tutu faced an uphill struggle in South Africa, and why today Christian activists face such problems in campaigning for the dropping of massive international debt, or the proper and humane treatment of asylum-seekers. It isn't just that vested financial and political interests have been ranged on the other side. It is that the entire climate of thought is against the church having anything to say on such subjects at all. God and Caesar belong in entirely separate compartments.

The excuse for reducing Christian content in public life, or indeed on radio or television, is always that religious minorities might be offended. But that's not the real reason, as the French ban on Muslim garb indicates. 'Tolerance', that much-vaunted but actually very hollow Enlightenment ideal, has nothing to do with the question. The real reason is the modernist ideology according to which religion is something for consenting adults in private, because God and the world simply don't mix. And that, to repeat, is not the *result* of modern physical or political science. It is its *presupposition*.

What then might the church have to say to all this? The Western church has by and large given up the idea of the kingdom of God, of God claiming his rightful sovereignty over the whole of creation. Generations have been schooled to read Jesus' language about the kingdom as referring, not to God's saving rule *over* creation, but to a heavenly kingdom into which God will receive those he has rescued *from* creation. And when Christians protest, as they sometimes do, about the banning of Christian symbols from the public sphere, they tend to argue from within the consensus rather than taking the harder route of understanding why the consensus is there in the first place and why and how it must be challenged. That is the problem, I think, with the current reaction to the New

Atheists. The reaction, or much of it, has happened within the same implicit structure of thought. But it's the structure that must be challenged.

The challenge must come, not in the name of the kind of 'theocracy' of which the Western world is so understandably afraid, but in the name of the utterly redefined and reshaped theocracy of which the four gospels speak. The crucifixion scene, in which Jesus is lifted up as king of the Jews and hence king of the world, is also the scene through which *power itself is redefined*. And it is in that redefinition of power that we may glimpse, as though for the first time, the vital, crucial and God-given place which the church, and Christian faith, can and must have in tomorrow's public life.

It isn't a matter, you see, of the church claiming a small slice of the ordinary kind of power. Actually, even in the UK where some bishops sit in the House of Lords, this isn't a matter of power, though that was clearly the case at one time. The way it works today is to ensure that the voice of the churches is heard in the discussion. But that's not the point; that's not, in any case, the kind of power which should concern a theocracy *remoulded around the cross of Jesus*. Jesus' kind of power looks completely different – not because it's 'spiritual' as opposed to 'worldly' or 'earthly' (that's the route to Gnosticism) but because it operates as a direct result of Jesus' own agenda, and of the cross with which that agenda reached its triumphant, if deeply paradoxical, conclusion.

Jesus' kind of power was set out, famously, in the Sermon on the Mount. But the Sermon too has often been misunderstood. When Jesus announces the Beatitudes, giving his blessing to certain kinds of people, we should remember what 'blessing' actually means. The 'Beatitudes' are Jesus' agenda for kingdom-people. They are not simply about how to behave so that God will do something nice *to* you. They are about the fact that Jesus wants to rule the world *through* you, but that for that to happen you'll have to become people of this kind. The Sermon on the Mount is a call to Jesus' followers to take up their vocation, which was the Israel-vocation that Jesus made his own: the vocation to be light to the world, to be salt to the earth – in other words, to be people through whom Jesus' kingdom-vision was to become a reality. The victory of Jesus over the powers of sin and death is to be implemented in the wider world through people like this.

The work of the kingdom, in fact, and with it the place of Jesus' followers in the public life of the world, is summed up pretty well in those Beatitudes. As I have often said, when God wants to change the world, he doesn't send in the tanks. He sends in the meek, the mourners, those who are hungry and thirsty for God's justice, the peacemakers, and so on. Just as God's whole *style*, his chosen way of operating, reflects his generous love, sharing his rule with his human creatures, so the way in which those humans then have to behave if they are to be agents of Jesus' lordship reflects in its turn the same sense of vulnerable, gentle but powerful self-giving love. It is because of this that the world has been changed (to refer to them once more) by people like William Wilberforce; by Desmond Tutu, working and praying not just to end apartheid but to end it in such a way as to produce a reconciled, forgiving South Africa; by Cicely Saunders, starting a hospice for terminally ill patients, initially ignored or scorned by the medical profession, but launching a movement that has, within a generation, spread right round the globe.

Jesus rules the world today by launching new initiatives that radically challenge the accepted ways of doing things: by Jubilee projects to remit ridiculous and unpayable debt, by housing trusts that provide accommodation for low-income families or homeless people, by local and sustainable agricultural projects that care for creation instead of destroying it in the hope of quick profit. And so on. We have domesticated the Christian idea of 'good works' so that it has simply become 'the keeping of ethical commands' – so that then people imagine that the place of Christian faith in public life will be a matter of imposing 'our standards' on everyone else. Instead, in the New Testament, 'good works' are what Christians are supposed to be doing in and for the wider community. Do good to *all* people, insists Paul, especially (of course) your fellow Christians (Galatians 6.10). *That is how the sovereignty of Jesus is put into effect.* Jesus went about feeding the hungry, curing the sick and rescuing lost sheep; his Body is supposed to be doing the same. That is how his kingdom is at work. The church, in fact, made its way in the world for many centuries by doing all this kind of thing. Now that in many countries the 'state' has assumed responsibility for many such areas of life (that's part of what I mean by saying that the state, not least in Western democracies, has become 'ecclesial', a kind of secular shadow-church) the church has been in danger of forgetting that these were its primary tasks all along.

This vision of the church's calling – to be the means through which Jesus continues to work and to teach, to establish his sovereign rule on earth as in heaven – is an ideal so high that it might seem not only unattainable and triumphalistic but hopelessly out of touch and in denial about its own sins and shortcomings. One of today's most-repeated clichés is that there are lots of people who find God believable but the church unbearable, Jesus appealing but the church appalling. We are never short of ecclesial follies and failings, as the sorrowing faithful and the salivating journalists know well. What does it mean to say that Jesus is King when the people who are supposed to be putting his kingship into practice are letting the side down so badly?

There are three things to say here, and each of them matters quite a lot. To begin with, for every Christian leader who ends up in court or in the newspapers there are hundreds and thousands who are doing a great job, unnoticed except within their own communities. The public only notices what gets into the papers, but the papers only report the odd and the scandalous, allowing sneering outsiders to assume that the church is collapsing into a little heap of squabbling factions. Mostly it isn't. The newspaper-perspective is like someone who only walks down a certain street on the one day a week when people put out their garbage for collection, and who then reports that the street is always full of garbage. Christians ought not to collude with the sneerers. Walk down the street some other time, we ought to say. Come and see us on a normal day.

Second, though, we must never forget that the way Jesus worked then and works now is through forgiveness and restoration. The church is not supposed to be a society of perfect people doing great work. It's a society of forgiven sinners repaying their own unpayable debt of love by working for Jesus' kingdom in every way they can, knowing themselves to be unworthy of the task. I suspect that part at least of the cause of the scandals is, as I suggested before, the triumphalism which allows some people to think that because of their baptism, or vocation, or ordination, or whatever, they are immune to serious sin – or that, if it happens, it must be an odd accident rather than a tell-tale sign of a serious problem.

But the third point is perhaps the most important, and it opens up a whole new area at which I glanced earlier on and to which we now return. The way in which Jesus exercises his sovereign lordship in the present time includes his strange, often secret, sovereignty over the nations and their rulers. God, insists the Bible, is at work in all sorts of ways in the world, whether or not people acknowledge him. But part of this belief is the belief that one of the church's primary roles is *to bear witness to the sovereign rule of Jesus, holding the world to account.* The church has a task which modern Western democracies have attempted to replicate in other ways. We have tried to produce, within our systems, some semblance of 'accountability'. If the voters don't like someone, they don't have to vote for him or her next time round. We all know that this is a very blunt instrument. Accountability isn't all it's cracked up to be. In the UK, most of the seats are 'safe', and most of the candidates are professional party hacks with little experience of real outside life.

So those who follow Jesus have the task, front and centre within their vocation, of being the real 'opposition'. This doesn't mean that they must actually 'oppose' everything that the government tries to do. They must weigh it, sift it, hold it to account, affirm what can be affirmed, point out things that are lacking or not quite in focus, critique what needs critiquing, and denounce, on occasion, what needs denouncing. It is telling that, in the early centuries of church history, the Christian bishops gained a reputation in the wider world for being the champions of the poor. They spoke up for their rights; they spoke out against those who would abuse and ill-treat them. Naturally: the bishops were followers of Jesus; they sang his mother's song; what else would you expect? That role continues to this day. And it goes much wider. The church has a wealth of experience, and centuries of careful reflection, in the fields of education, health care, the treatment of the elderly, the needs and vulnerabilities of refugees and migrants, and so on. We should draw on this experience and use it to full effect.

This facet of the church's 'witness', this central vocation through which Jesus continues his work to this day, has been marginalized. Modern Western democracies haven't wanted to be held to account in this way, and so have either officially or unofficially driven a fat wedge between 'church' and 'state'. (The newspapers have joined in, as the self-appointed 'unofficial opposition'; they, too, have therefore a vested interest in keeping the church off their patch.) But, as we have hinted already, this has actually changed the meanings of the words 'church' and 'state'. 'State' has expanded to do some of what 'church' should be doing; and the churches themselves have colluded with the privatization of 'religion', leaving all the things that the church used to do best at to 'the state' or other agencies. No wonder, when people within the church speak up or speak out on key issues of the day, those who don't like what they say tell them to go back to their private 'religious' world.

But speak up, and speak out, we must, because we have not only the clear instruction of Jesus himself but the clear promise that *this is how he will exercise his sovereignty; this is how he will make his kingdom a reality.* In John's gospel Jesus tells his followers that the Spirit will call the world to account. This is central to Christian vocation, but for most it remains a closed book. Inevitably, the church will sometimes get it wrong. If the church is to exercise a prophetic gift towards the world, this will require further prophetic ministries within the church itself, to challenge, confront and correct, as well as to endorse, what has been said, and so to ensure the good standing of the church itself.

This, then, is a central and often ignored part of the meaning of Jesus' kingdom for today. Each generation, and each local church, needs to pray for its civic leaders. Granted the wide variety of forms of government, types of constitution and so forth that obtain across the world, each generation, and each local church, needs to figure out wise and appropriate ways of speaking the truth to power. *That is a central part of the present-day meaning of Jesus' universal Kingship.*

We can sum it all up like this. We live in the period of Jesus' sovereign rule over the world – a reign that is not yet complete, since as Paul says, 'he must reign until he has put all his enemies under his feet', including death itself (1 Corinthians 15.20–28). But Paul is clear: we do not have to wait until the second coming to say that Jesus is already reigning. In trying to understand this present 'reign' of Jesus, though, we have seen two apparently quite different strands. On the one hand, we have seen that all the powers and authorities in the universe are now, in some sense or other, subject to Jesus. This doesn't mean that they all do what he wants all the time; only that Jesus intends that there should be social and political structures of governance, and that he will hold them to account. We should not be shy about recognizing – however paradoxical it seems to our black-and-white minds! – the God-givenness of structures of authority, even when they are tyrannous, violent and in need of radical reformation. We in the modern West have trained ourselves to think of political legitimacy simply in terms of the method or mode of appointment: once people have voted, that confers 'legitimacy'. The ancient Jews and early Christians, by contrast, were not particularly interested in how rulers had come to be rulers. They were far more interested in holding rulers responsible in terms of what they were actually doing once in power. God wants rulers; but God will call them to account.

Where does Jesus come into all this? From his own perspective, he was both upstaging the power structures of his day and also calling them to account, right then and there. But his death, resurrection and ascension were the demonstration that he was Lord and the powers and authorities were not. The calling-to-account has, in other words, already begun. It will be completed at the second coming. *And the church's work of speaking the truth to power means what it means because it is based on the first of these and anticipates the second.* What the church does, in the power of the Spirit, is rooted in the achievement of Jesus and looks ahead to the final completion of his work. This is how Jesus is running the world in the present.

But, happily, it doesn't stop there. There is more to the church's vocation than the constant critique, both positive and negative, of what the world's rulers are getting up to. There are millions of things which the church should be getting stuck into that the rulers of the world either don't bother about or don't have the resources or the political will to support. Jesus has all kinds of projects up his sleeve and is simply waiting for faithful people to say their prayers, to read the signs of the times, and to get busy. Nobody would have dreamed of a 'Truth and Reconciliation Commission' if Desmond Tutu hadn't prayed and pushed and made it happen. Nobody would have worked out the Jubilee movement, to campaign for international debt relief, if people in the churches had not become serious about the ridiculous plight of the poor. Closer to home, nobody else is likely to volunteer to play the piano for the service at the local prison. Few other people will start a play-group for the children of single mothers who are still at work when school finishes. Nobody else, in my experience, will listen to the plight of isolated rural communities or equally isolated inner-city enclaves. Nobody else thought of organizing the 'Street

Pastors' scheme which, in the UK at least, has had a remarkable success in reducing crime and gently but firmly pointing out to aimless young people that there is a different way to be human. And so on. And so on.

And if the response is that these things are all very small and, in themselves, insignificant, I reply in two ways. First, didn't Jesus explain his own actions by talking about the smallest of the seeds that then grows into the largest kind of shrub? And second, haven't we noticed how one small action can start a trend? That's how the hospice movement spread, transforming within a generation the care of terminally ill patients. *Jesus is at work, taking forward his kingdom-project.*

He is, no doubt, doing this in a million ways of which we see little. The cosmic vision of Colossians is true, and should give us hope, not least when we have to stand before local government officials and explain what we were doing praying for people on the street, or why we need to rent a public hall for a series of meetings, or why we remain implacably opposed to a new business that is seeking shamelessly to exploit young people or low-income families. When we explain ourselves, we do so before people who, whether they know it or not, have been appointed to their jobs by God himself. Jesus has, on the cross, defeated the power that they might have over us. And, as we pray, and proclaim Jesus' death in the sacraments, we claim that victory and go to our work calmly and without fear.

This is, after all, what Jesus himself told us to expect. The poor in spirit will be making the kingdom of heaven happen. The meek will be taking over the earth, so gently that the powerful won't notice until it's too late. The peacemakers will be putting the arms manufacturers out of business. Those who are hungry and thirsty for God's justice will be analysing government policy and legal rulings and speaking up on behalf of those at the bottom of the pile. The merciful will be surprising everybody by showing that there is a different way to do human relations: some people know only how to be judgmental, to give as good as they get, to lash out and get their own back, but the Beatitude-people will unveil, and by their example they will encourage, a refreshingly different way. You are the light of the world, said Jesus. You are the salt of the earth. He was announcing a programme yet to be completed. He was inviting his hearers, then and now, to join him in making it happen. This is what it looks like when Christian faith is doing its job within the public life of today's and tomorrow's world. My hope and prayer is that in Ireland, as in Britain and America, we will be able to work through the present troubles, sorrows and scandals. Ireland was once the teacher of the world in matters of faith and life. May it be so again.

10

Jesus and the kingdom of God, then and now

If you went out on the street in the City of London and asked a random passer-by what Jesus had to say that might be relevant to today's world, among the colourful answers you might receive someone would probably quote Mark 12.17. In the UK it tends to be people on the right who quote it, and in the USA people on the left; but it still serves the same purpose. 'Render unto Caesar the things that are Caesar's', they will say, 'and to God the things that are God's.' End of conversation, so they think: a nice big church–state split. You Christians get on and say your prayers and go to heaven, and we will run the world down here by Caesar's rules. And among the ironies and muddles of using *that text* to make that point is the fact that when Jesus said it it was a sharp answer making almost exactly the opposite point. And I begin with this, plunging into the heart of our subject, because here we see, close up and dangerous, two things that Jesus was all about, which the gospels do their best to bring out but which our modern readings usually obscure. What was going on?

It was clearly a trick question: Should we or shouldn't we pay tribute to Caesar? Taxes were just as hot a topic in Jesus' day as they are now, but even more so then, first because they were imposed by the hated Romans, and second because already, when Jesus was a boy, there had been anti-tax riots leading to brutal repression, including crucifixions. Bad memories sharpened the question to a poisoned tip. If he says, 'Pay the tax', we'll know that all his talk about the kingdom of God is about as useful as a dead sheep. If he says, 'Don't pay the tax', the first-century radicals will love him but the authorities will have him on toast. But what they don't realize is that Jesus can tap into older memories as well. Two hundred years earlier, still powerful in folk memory, Judas Maccabaeus and his brothers had mounted a daring and successful revolt against the previous imperial regime, that of Syria. And their watchword was: *Pay back the Gentiles as they deserve, and keep God's commandments* (1 Maccabees 2.68). Pay back Caesar what he's got coming to him? What sort of a quisling slogan is that? Jesus asks for a coin. All right, he says: *You'd better pay Caesar back in his own coin; and pay God back in his own coin!* This is nothing to do with a church–state split. Yes, Caesar has a legitimate claim – up to a point, and perhaps at some point he needs to be confronted, though not in the way you'd normally imagine. But the claim of God, whose image is borne not just by coins but by every living human being – this claim overrides, supersedes, trumps and upstages all other claims. Sure, it's a trick answer to a trick question. But when you put it in historical context it is anything but a mandate for a modernist split of religion and politics. As we see in Jesus' trial before Pontius Pilate, Pilate does have some legitimate authority. But God will hold all authorities accountable for what they do with that delegated vocation.

So here are the two things that Mark and the others want to bring out, which our modern readings have all but obscured. First, when Jesus talked about the kingdom of God he really did mean that this was the time for God to become king, to take his power and reign in a whole new way, a way which would not merely challenge Caesar's kingdom but would challenge Caesar's *type* of kingdom. Second, Jesus was consciously drawing on to himself, and his vocation, the weight of Israel's ancient tradition. But what have modern readings done with all this? First, we have turned the gospel *narrative* about a world-shattering *event* into fragments of teaching about a new *religion*, complete with cute little ethical maxims. Second, we have come to the text with our modern assumption that religion and politics have nothing to do with one another, and we have read that modern dogma into the story whether it makes sense or not. And frankly it doesn't and can't make sense; because the whole meaning of God's kingdom, going back through the Psalms and the Prophets all the way to the Torah itself, is about the one true God calling time on the wicked empires of the world and setting up a radically different kind of empire instead. And the modern split-world dogma has radically affected scholarship, preaching and popular assumptions in ways too numerous to mention here.

Let's jump to a different but equally well-known example: the story of the so-called Prodigal Son. Rembrandt painted it; preachers and spiritual directors use it all the time; millions of humble souls have quite rightly found in it a wonderful encouragement to come back from the far country to a father's overflowingly generous welcome. Yes, of course. But there is so much more going on here. For a start, Jesus is plugging in to one of the oldest biblical themes: the young son who goes off into the far country and returns to find his older brother less than fully happy about it. Think of Jacob and Esau. But think, as well, of the powerful story of the second-Temple Jewish world: of the horribly elongated time of 'exile', not just geographically in Babylon, but, as Daniel 9 insisted, a kind of political and theological exile going on and on for half a millennium. What will it look like when this 'exile' is finally over? In Daniel, as in Isaiah, the ultimate return from exile is all about God becoming king – that theme again: and Jesus is saying, It's here! It's happening before your eyes! Look: this your brother was dead and is alive again; he was lost and he's found! As with so many of Jesus' parables, the point is not 'an earthly story with a heavenly meaning'.

This is part of our problem: we have domesticated these powerful stories, so that the wonderful meaning they rightly have for us as individuals is all the meaning we allow them, which is to miss the larger point. Often, when Jesus was telling stories, particularly stories rather obviously coded to carry a message about God and what he was up to in the story of Israel, this wasn't to give abstract teaching about God, or heaven, for its own sake. It was to explain what he, Jesus, was up to at the time. *Why are you eating and celebrating with all the wrong people?* they asked him. Answer: Once upon a time there was a shepherd who lost one sheep . . . there was a woman who lost a coin . . . there was a father who had two sons (Luke 15).

Again, in its first-century context, the message is both comforting and disturbing. Who is this older brother who doesn't want the father to welcome the younger one back? People used to sneer that Jesus told stories about God but that the early church spoke about Jesus instead, as if the church were sneakily divinizing him in retrospect. Not so. Jesus told those stories, these God-stories, these God-and-Israel stories, *in order to explain what he himself was doing*. Something was *happening*, then and there. This was never simply timeless spiritual teaching, though it transports brilliantly across all times and cultures. This was about the unique event taking place in Jesus' public career. That is what our modern world, and often our modern church, has not wanted to hear. But it's what the gospels are saying, and it's what Jesus was *doing*.

Or take a third rather obvious example. Jesus came to Jerusalem one last time, and he did something in the Temple which caused some frantic reactions and led quite quickly to his arrest and his death. We've often called this incident 'the cleansing of the Temple', and we've interpreted it in terms of Jesus trying to clean up Jerusalem's religion, to purge it of commercialism, and so forth. But the four gospels make it clear, in interestingly different ways, that it was far, far more than that. It was Passover time: liberation time, time for God to overthrow the pharaohs of this world and set his people free. The Jewish people then and now knew and know the Passover story better than most of us know the Christmas and Easter stories. They would know that in the book of Exodus the point of Israel being freed from Egypt was so that they could worship their God in the desert and then come into their inheritance. And the book of Exodus ends magnificently, after some horrible moments on the way, with the construction of the Tabernacle, and the glorious divine presence coming to dwell in it. Exodus 40 echoes Genesis 1 and 2, and that's quite deliberate: this is a new creation, a microcosmos, the consolidation of the promise to Abraham that in his family all the families of the earth would be blessed. That's what the exodus is all about: God is rescuing his people, and coming to dwell in their midst, so that they can be his royal priesthood.

And Passover isn't just a story. It's a festival, with liturgy and hymns and dramatic actions, focused on the Temple and the meal, and praying for the ultimate coming of God's kingdom, for God to be king over all the world as the Psalms had said and as Miriam sang beside the sea. So when Jesus came to Jerusalem and performed his dramatic action in the Temple, bringing the sacrificial system to a shuddering halt for a short but deeply symbolic moment, and then taking his followers off for a private meal that both was and wasn't like the ordinary Passover meal, he was saying something far more powerfully through these combined and contextualized symbols than any words could convey. He was saying, This is the time, this is the place, this is how the ultimate Passover is happening, the new exodus, the real return from exile. This is how the kingdom of God is coming – and its focus will not be on this temple of stone and timber but on a different kind of temple altogether. Jesus had acted, throughout his public career, as if he was the Temple in person. If you wanted forgiveness or healing, you came to him. Now even Jerusalem itself wasn't big enough for both of them. He had his eye on the prize: if I by the finger of God cast out demons, he had said, then God's kingdom has arrived, has come upon you (Luke 11.20 and the parallel in Matthew 12.28).

What, after all, was a Messiah supposed to do? Different traditions of the time said different things, but at their heart we get the general answers: a Messiah must fulfil the scriptures, must defeat the ultimate enemies, must rebuild or cleanse the Temple so that Israel's God can come back there in glory, and must establish God's reign not only over Israel but over the world. This is a vision of radical cosmic renewal, and we have turned it into religion. This is a story of a world set free, of humans set free, and we have turned it into psychotherapy on the one hand or personal ethics on the other – vital in their place, but woefully inadequate if substituted for the big picture. Jesus believed that it was his calling to liberate Israel and the world once and for all from the grip of the darkest of enemies, and to set up the new microcosmos, the new Tabernacle, the dwelling place of the living God, made not from stone and timber but from living, breathing human beings, with himself as the ultimate human, the son of man, suffering at the hands of the monsters as in Daniel 7 but then exalted to the right hand of the majesty on high. Never forget: when Jesus wanted to explain to his closest followers what his forthcoming death was all about, he didn't give them a theory; he gave them a meal.

Now even if you think that Jesus was totally mistaken; that his dreams died with him; that Christianity as we know it is based on a tragic mistake or simply wishful thinking – then you must still admit that this vision of a new reality coming to birth remains noble and powerful. I have argued in detail elsewhere that this picture is thoroughly historically credible. Jesus of Nazareth was not teaching a new 'religion' – even granted that the word 'religion' meant something quite different then anyway. Nor was he telling people the secret about how they could go to heaven after they died. He has remarkably little to say about that, since his message was not about people going to heaven but about heaven – the rule of heaven, and in himself the very presence of heaven – coming to earth. Nor was he coming to launch just another ordinary protest movement, though when we grasp what the gospels are saying there will be a new energy and sense of direction for a good deal of protest. Nor was he offering simply a way to reorder your private interiority, though when you are grasped by his message, and sign on to take up his cross, it will indeed turn you upside down and inside out, some of which will be wonderfully comforting and some of which, as he warned, will be profoundly discomforting. He was claiming to inaugurate God's sovereign rule on earth as in heaven – in other words, a form of theocracy. But, whereas that very word sends shivers down our Western democratic spines, not least because of other recent theocratic experiments of both left and right, the whole point was that what Jesus was claiming was a *cruciform theocracy*: the inauguration of God's sovereign, saving rule, on earth as in heaven, by means of the cross.

This is where our modern world – and much of the modern church – rebels angrily. We got rid of that nonsense in the eighteenth century, we're told; we don't want it back again! What has happened, in a nutshell, is that the basic Epicureanism of the Enlightenment – the idea of a split world with the gods away up in the attic and the world progressing under its own steam down here – has been so taken for granted that all our reading of the gospels, all our thinking about Jesus and his message, all our public and political life, all our theorizing about morals and meaning and marriage and mysticism and much besides, has been forced into that framework, as on to a Procrustean bed. And the gospels themselves tell us that this is wrong. We are falsifying the record. That's just not what was going on. Naturally, secularism doesn't want theocracy at any price. But the churches have gone along with this, colluding with the idea of the God–Caesar split, consenting to look after people's eternal destinies and leaving the politicians to run the planet. That is why, so often, the meaning of the cross has shifted dramatically, from being the extraordinary way in which the living God wins the ultimate victory over the powers to being simply the mechanism for dealing with individual sins. Obviously, dealing with sins is pretty important as well. That is actually part of the means by which the cosmic victory is won. That's a topic for another time.

And of course all this only escapes the charge of wishful thinking if it ends with Jesus' victory. The church so often hasn't known what to do with Easter. We have oscillated between demythologizing it into the rise of faith among Jesus' disappointed followers and making it simply the glorious miracle at the end of a sad story, proving that God really can do powerful tricks and that we really will go to heaven after all. Neither of those will do. The bodily resurrection of Jesus is the only thing that will explain, historically, why the church got going and took the shape it did. I have argued that elsewhere. Questions abound, and I'm happy to deal with them, but for the moment I assume that argument and move to the vital result.

Even if you're going to decide that the gospels are telling a pack of well-meaning lies (or even ill-meaning lies!), at least let us be clear what it is they are saying. They are not offering Jesus as a magic man, a Superman-figure doing tricks to con people into adopting a new religion. They are not talking about Jesus as a first-century Che Guevara, a bearded revolutionary offering a socialist Utopia. They are not giving us Jesus as an ethical teacher, a moral example, a spiritual guru or even, taken out of context, an atoning sacrifice. They are not presenting us with a Jesus who simply makes us feel good about ourselves. All of those point to some elements in his teaching, but any of them, when isolated, distorts, and distorts radically. The point is – and the resurrection enables us to say this without the ifs and buts – with Jesus *something happened because of which the world is a different place.*

It isn't different in the way we might have wanted or expected. It certainly isn't different in the way that Jesus' Jewish contemporaries wanted or expected. But as the four gospels tell it, and as I think Jesus himself intended it, something happened in those thirty years, and in the three days at their climax, because of which it makes vital sense to speak of new creation; it makes sense to speak of the new Temple; it makes sense to speak of a new humanity. And it makes sense, above all, not just to speak of it but to live it, to sign on, to hear the call of Jesus right now to be part of his kingdom-project, to recognize, as Bonhoeffer said, that when Christ calls you he bids you come and die, to die in baptism, to die to the sin which seems so vital and central a part of you, to die to the social and cultural and intellectual and political expectations that swirl in their dangerous currents around you, and to follow instead into the new life with kingdom-tasks to perform and with Jesus himself leading the way. All this makes sense: a new kind of sense, perhaps, but sense none the less.

That is how the resurrection narratives in the four gospels leave us, and I'll come back to that in a moment. But let me say something first about how the gospels work. I am here standing on the shoulders of other recent scholars on the gospels, such as Richard Burridge in his work on the gospels as biographies and Richard Hays on the echoes of scripture in the gospels. But I still think most ordinary churchgoers, and a great many who study and teach the gospels, have not begun to come to terms with the multi-layered story they tell. Face it, human life is multi-layered: put together love and art and food and drink and politics and philosophy and shopping and science and monarchy and money and war and death ... most of that is going on in our minds and bodies most of the time, and we shouldn't be surprised if, like a great symphonic poem, the gospels are themselves multi-layered, working in several dimensions at once. This is the danger of our churchly (and perhaps personal) practice of reading the gospels in small segments. When we know how to do it that will still work; I began with three such fragments at the start of this chapter. But we need the larger narrative. And I offer you four basic strands which all come rushing together, in different ways, in the four gospels.

First, the gospels all tell the story of Jesus as the story of how Israel's story reached its intended climax. Ludwig Wittgenstein said that the Hebrew scriptures offer us a torso, and the gospels offer us the head for that torso. They affirm the ancient Hebrew story even while affirming that this is where it was supposed to lead. This was how the ancient dream of the sovereign and rescuing rule of the creator God had to come about. The gospels achieve this in many and various ways, weaving together Torah, prophecy and psalms not as isolated proof-texts but as the single great story, summed up in the apocalyptic language of Daniel in terms of the four pagan kingdoms to be followed by the establishment of God's kingdom, and in terms of the extended exile that will at last be undone through the dark events of the abomination of desolation and the fate of the anointed one.

Second, simultaneously, the gospels all tell the story of Jesus as the story of how the radically new community – and yet in radical continuity with the family of Abraham – was launched upon the world. They do not describe the founding of a new 'religion', another 'ism', but rather of the launching, modelling and making of a new way of being human.

Third, and most startling still, the four gospels – all of them, not only John – tell the story of Jesus as the story of *how Israel's God fulfilled his long promise to return in person to rescue the world and make his home within it.* Clearly, this depends – as the gospels recognize – on the further point, that the risen Jesus is now somehow, strangely, already in charge of this world. Once more we can invoke the words Matthew ascribes to the risen Jesus: all authority in heaven *and on earth* has been given to him. And it also depends on the assumption that the risen Jesus gives his own powerful Spirit to his followers to enable them to be his people in and for the world. But the point is that what was later called 'incarnation', the embodiment of Israel's God in the person of Jesus, was deep within the story from the very start. A great many clergy, never mind anybody else, were taught something very different from this in college, and it's time to read our texts afresh.

Fourth, as we have hinted, the narrative of Israel's God coming back in person to bring Israel's story to its climax must inevitably be the story of the final great clash between the creator God and the idolatrous empires of the world. That is the story we find in Exodus, in the Psalms (especially Psalm 2), in Isaiah 40—55 and in Daniel – all of them central to the gospels' account of Jesus, and all of them arguably central to Jesus' own sense of vocation. To read this story in an apolitical or anti-political manner is to falsify it before you start. Hence my reading of the 'God and Caesar' saying earlier on.

The gospels therefore bring together and hold together, without any sense of strain or strangeness, what both the church and the watching world have found it remarkably difficult to combine: the kingdom and the cross. When I was in Durham I knew many clergy and parishes who focused on the kingdom: here is Jesus, feeding the hungry and rescuing the outcast; we'll go and do the same. (But then, the puzzle: what a pity he died so young!) And I knew many other clergy and parishes where the focus was on the cross: Jesus died for our sins so that we could go to heaven. (And then, the opposite puzzle: for them, it would have been sufficient if Jesus had been born of a virgin and died on a cross and never done anything much in between – which means that Matthew, Mark, Luke and John were wasting their time.) This dilemma is a tell-tale symptom of the whole problem of post-Enlightenment Western Christianity. The gospels tell the story of how the cross wins the victory of the kingdom, the messianic victory; and, conversely, of how the kingdom came, and comes – not in the manner of earthly kingdoms, but in a different way altogether. Cruciform theocracy again. The rulers of the world do it one way, said Jesus, but we're going to do it the other way. Power stood on its head. If only the church had taken that seriously all along.

I promised to say something in conclusion about what all this might mean for us today. For me, the biggest battle is always to get people to grasp the idea of what in the trade we call *inaugurated eschatology*: that something *happened* in Jesus' kingdom-launching activity, in his death, resurrection and ascension – something because of which the world is a radically different place, with new possibilities especially for human vocation, life and destiny. The Enlightenment has hated that message, because its own claim has been that nothing really happened with Jesus, except some new religious options for those so inclined, and that the real turning-point of history was its own moment, the rise of modern science and democracy. That clash stands behind many of our puzzles today, not least because, let me hasten to add, I believe that science and democracy are in principle God-given blessings.

But they are not the kingdom of God. Where I see the gospel, and the gospels, biting today at the macro level has to do with the way in which Western society has bought so deeply into the narratives of the Enlightenment, and then cannot understand what's gone wrong when the tragedies of the world quite literally wash up on our shores as they have recently been doing. What we see today, with the refugee crisis, is in part the result of horribly bad decisions over the last two decades, and in particular our failure to understand the *narrative*. We have told ourselves a story about getting rid of tyrants so that peace, love, flower-power and Western democracy can flourish automatically. How naive could we be? Instead, the gospel vision of a world under the gentle and wise rule of Jesus – think of the Sermon on the Mount – tells a very different story. Read Psalm 72 if you want the biblical pattern of human rule: the needs of the poor and helpless are the absolute priority, and those whose actions have unwittingly made more people poor and helpless ought to be first in the line to help. The postmodernists are right: the big stories of modernism have let us down. But postmodernity has no new story to put in its place, and hates the very idea of such a thing. We have such a story; but it's a love story, not a power story. We must both model it ourselves and urge it upon our rulers as the only way forward.

So too with the other great postmodern critiques, truth and power and self. Read John 18 and 19 and see Jesus arguing with Pontius Pilate about kingdom, truth and power; then put that template upon the wastes of our present wraths and sorrows. From a gospel point of view, 'truth' is the word which humans speak which brings God's order into the world. But the 'truth' in question is not just the 'truth' of the old creation, readily dressed up as cynicism, but the truth of the *new* creation, which takes fully into account the tragedies and horrors of the present old world while also speaking the word of healing and freedom which opens the way to the resurrection life of the new creation here and now.

As for power, when people say (as they often do), 'Why doesn't God *do* something?', they always seem to assume that if God was really in control he'd send in the tanks and stop the bullies and the unscrupulous getting away with it. But according to the Sermon on the Mount (and it was the Sermon on the Mount's agenda which Jesus was fulfilling when he went to his death, going the second mile carrying his Roman cross, turning the other cheek to his mockers, and ending up on a hill where he could not be hidden), when God wants to change the world he doesn't send in the tanks. As we saw in the previous chapter, he sends in the meek, the mourners, the merciful, the hungry-for-justice people, the peacemakers, the incorruptibly pure in heart. That was never a list of qualities you needed to try to work at in order to get to heaven. It was always a list of human characteristics *through which God would bring his kingdom on earth as in heaven*. That is how God works. And by the time the bullies and the arrogant have woken up to what's happening, the meek and the mourners and the merciful have built hospitals and schools; they are looking after the sick and the wounded; they are feeding the hungry and rescuing the helpless; and they are telling the powerful and the vested-interest people that this is what a genuinely human society looks like, thank you very much.

Thank God that this is what the church has been doing from the very beginning. Thank God for all those who are working at the sharp end of this project right now. Often our grasp of vocation is stronger than our understanding of the integrated theological message of the gospels that in fact underlies it; but this integrated message will strengthen and direct us as we go to these tasks, and in particular will help us in that specifically Christian responsibility, speaking this truth to power.

The newspapers hate us doing that, naturally, since they are convinced that speaking the truth to power is their job. So they, like the politicians, want us to go on saying our prayers and keeping out of their way. But of course the more we say our prayers – with 'thy kingdom come on earth as in heaven' at the heart of them! – the more we cannot refrain from speaking as Jesus did to Pilate, even if they crucify us for it.

And what about the 'self', that great bastion of modernity and object of postmodern deconstruction? Out of that muddle has come a great and often unhealthy obsession, once more, not only with 'self' but also with 'identity', leading to much misunderstanding. Often people suppose that the point of the Christian message is to 'affirm' our 'identities' of whatever sort. That comes from Gnosticism, not from the gospel. Jesus spoke of losing one's self in order to find it. The gospels are written in such a way that they draw us into that losing-and-finding dynamic, where nothing remains the same except the Father's love. There is much more to be said down that line, but not now.

I have written elsewhere about the way in which the four gospels, and particularly John's gospel, close with the challenge to Jesus' followers to go out into the world with a new kind of mission. The gospels are telling the story of new creation, of a new temple, of new life, of kingdom and cross and resurrection, of scripture fulfilled and heaven come to earth. This massive narrative comes to each one of us like a tidal wave, to scoop us up into its sweep and substance. And when we say, as we are bound to do, 'No, I'm not ready, I'm not up for all that, it's too much, I can't grasp it, anyway I'm afraid . . .' Jesus says to us, as he said in effect to Peter in John 21: 'That's OK; if that's where you are, that's where we'll start. Now: follow me.'

I hope I have made clear, in this very brief discussion of Jesus and the gospels, that at their heart the gospels tell a story which much of the Western world – including sadly the church! – has all but forgotten. This is the story, not of the founding of a new religion, not merely of Jesus as a moral or religious hero to be imitated, not of a new way of escaping this world and going to heaven, not of a way of being comfortable in our skins, but of Jesus of Nazareth as Israel's Messiah and the world's true Lord, the living and loving embodiment of the one true and living God, launching God's kingdom on earth as in heaven by his public career, his death, resurrection and ascension, and calling men, women and children everywhere to share his life, to be rescued by his death, to celebrate his resurrection and to live under his ascended lordship. Our prayer must be, for the church in its vital witness to all this as the world moves through the turbulent and uncharted waters of the twenty-first century: that those who find themselves grasped by the message and love of Jesus may hear that summons, and by his Spirit play their parts, whatever they are, in the work Jesus has for his people in these difficult and dangerous days.

Acknowledgments

As I said in the Preface, I am very grateful to those whose kind invitations gave me the opportunity to think through these ideas in fresh ways for fresh contexts, and whose warm welcome and hospitality made the various occasions enjoyable as well as stimulating.

Paul and the Bible in tomorrow's world
Dr Perse's Sermon, Gonville and Caius College, Cambridge, February 2008

The Bible and the postmodern world
Orange Memorial Lecture, Christchurch, New Zealand, August 1999

Pilate, Caesar and Bible truth
St Andrews University Distance Learning Programme, September 2010

God, the earthly powers and terror
Durham Cathedral, November 2006

Power, faith and the law
London School of Economics, February 2008

God, power and human flourishing
The Squance Lecture, Sedbergh School, November 2008

God's powerful foolishness in a world of foolish power
Elmbrook Church, Milwaukee, November 2012

Christian virtue in peace and war
William Wright Memorial Lecture, The Royal Military Academy, Sandhurst, October 2010

Christian faith in public life
The C. S. Lewis Lecture, Dublin, October 2011

Jesus and the kingdom of God, then and now
St Paul's Cathedral, London, October 2015

Index of Scripture and ancient sources

Index of names and subjects

Did you know that SPCK is a registered charity?

As well as publishing great books by leading Christian authors, we also . . .

. . . **make assemblies meaningful and fun for over a million children** by running www.assemblies.org.uk, a popular website that provides free assembly scripts for teachers. For many children, school assembly is the only contact they have with Christian faith and culture, and the only time in their week for spiritual reflection.

. . . **help prisoners to become confident readers** with our easy-to-read stories. Poor literacy is a huge barrier to rehabilitation. Prisoners identify with the believable heroes of our gritty fiction. At the same time, questions at the end of each chapter help them to examine their choices from a moral perspective and to build their reading confidence.

. . . **support student ministers overseas in their training** through partnerships in the Global South.

Please support these great schemes: visit www.spck.org.uk/support-us to find out more.